SUCCESS YOURSELF

Also by John Mattone

How to Conduct Win-Win Performance Appraisals

Also by Richard Andersen

Arranging Deck Chairs on the Titanic: Crises in Education

Getting Ahead: Career Skills That Work

Déjà Vu All Over Again: The Last of the Great Sports Quotation Books

Master Microsoft Word: An Easy Guide for Effective Word Processing

Muckaluck: A Curious Episode in the Cavalry's Winning of the West

On the Run: The Fabulous Story of Felix Carvajal

Power Write! A Practical Guide to Words That Work

Robert Coover

Straight Cut Ditch

The Red Aristocrats: Michael and Catherine Karolyi

The Reluctant Hero and the Massachusetts 54th Colored Regiment

The Write Stuff: A Practical Guide to Style and Mechanics

William Goldman

Write It Right! An Essential Guide to Clear and Correct Writing

Writing That Works: A Practical Guide for Business

SUCCESS YOURSELF

Using the Enneagram to Unleash Your Personal and Business Potential

John Mattone and Richard Andersen

MasterMedia Limited ◢◣◣◣ **New York, New York**

Library of Congress Cataloging-in-Publications Data

Mattone, John and Andersen, Richard
Success yourself: using the Enneagram to unleash
your personal and business potential /
John Mattone and Richard Andersen

p. cm.
ISBN 1-57101-067-X : $21.95

MASTERMEDIA and colophon
are registered trademarks of MasterMedia Limited.

CIP: 96-076085
Design by Cranston Communications, Inc.
Manufactured in the United States of America

Dedications

From John:

*To Gayle, my loving wife and guiding force in my life,
and to my four children, Jared, Nick, Krissy and Matthew,
for their love and support. I love you all so much!*

From Richard:

*To my family and to the memory of my father, Arnold.
Takk For Alt.*

Acknowledgments

This book originated from four sources: constant travel over the last 10 years; research; consulting; and personal experiences. My speaking and consulting work has put me in contact with all types of people all over the world. I listened, I observed, and gave assistance when needed. This book reflects the essence of what I have learned about human nature. I want to share it with you.

This book was truly a team effort. I want to thank my wife, Gayle, and our four children—Jared 14, Nick 11, Krissy 7, and Matthew 4—your love is my strength. My Mom, who finally lost a courageous battle to cancer during the writing of this book—I miss you so much. My Dad, my personal hero—thanks for everything—I love you.

To my good friend and coauthor, Richard Andersen, a gifted writer and individual. You were an incredible source of writing brainpower and professional candor.

To Tony Colao, director of the Speaker's Bureau at MasterMedia, who has always believed in me and provided the emotional support and encouragement necessary to pursue my personal and professional goals—with passion. Tony is a source of inspiration.

To my assistant, Libby Harrison, who was devoted to the vision that what I was doing would make a difference. This book would not have been completed without her unswerving faithfulness.

To our editor, Virginia Koenke Hunt, who made sure we crossed all the *t*'s, dotted all the *i*'s and got all the arrows pointing in the right directions.

To my clients (and good friends), Ekkehard Grampp and Cindy Yates of Rohm Tech; John Liccardi of AT&T; John Rivera of Norwest Mortgage; Mark Eccher and Nick Riso of Nestle USA; Tonya Satryb of the State University of New York at Brockport; Norma Sanchez of Sonoco Products; Roseanne Brennan of Prime

Hospitality Corp.; Chuck Kopf of BIC Corporation; and Kathleen Webster of the Augusta (Maine) Mental Health Institute. Thank you so much for your support.

To the participants who have attended my speeches and seminars, I have learned much from you and acknowledge you for your participation in this work.

No one writes a book alone. I wish to acknowledge the contribution others have made to my life by freely sharing their thoughts. It is my sincere desire that you will benefit from the ideas and thoughts in this book and share them with others. Remember—it doesn't matter what you *can* do—what matters most is what you *will* do!

JOHN MATTONE
August 1996

Table of Contents

Introduction

We all want to become better family members and more proficient at work. Yet we fear change because change means destruction. In order for something new to take place, something current has to be destroyed.

Change also involves risk. What if the change isn't as effective as we had hoped? What if we fail? What if the people who depend on us are diminished in some way because of the action we took to improve ourselves?

And what about those areas of our lives where we're content? Where we have no desire to change but realize that unless we do, our competition will pass us by or our family members will reject us in some way?

The single great advantage of the Enneagram is that it helps us understand ourselves—the first and most important step for change. It also helps us understand others in ways both practical and profound. Understanding ourselves and others not only reduces the risk that change requires, but it also allows us to recognize and improve upon what we value most. And unlike every other human personality graphic, the Enneagram is *dynamic*. It doesn't just identify behaviors and tell you how to respond to them: It shows you how to improve your behavior in areas that will enrich your life; it reveals how you can eliminate from your behavior actions that are detrimental to you and the people who are important to you.

The world's single, most comprehensive system for understanding human nature, the Enneagram will show you in specific detail how to correct self-defeating neuroses and provide the map you need to reach your full potential as a human being: in other words, to become the person you know yourself to be.

JOHN MATTONE
RICHARD ANDERSEN

PART I

THE ENNEAGRAM

Chapter 1
Why You Need the Enneagram

Once upon a relatively short time ago, there was very little change during any person's lifetime. Consider, for example, the field of transportation. In BC 6000, the fastest form of group transportation on land was the camel caravan. Camels travel at about eight miles per hour. By 1784, the most popular form of group transportation was the stagecoach. Stagecoaches travel at an average speed of 10 miles per hour. It took humans almost 7,000 years to increase their group rate of speed by only two miles per hour! But then, in 1825, something happened: The steam engine was invented. By the end of the decade, locomotives carried people at an average speed of 13 miles per hour. In less than 50 years, we experienced a greater increase in our rate of speed than we did in the previous 7,000! Now skip ahead about a hundred years to 1938. Airplanes were carrying people at 100 miles an hour, and the very thought that, by 1960, missiles would transport astronauts at 1800 miles per hour was considered pure science fiction. Today, of course, an 1800 mph missile is a relic.

This tremendous rate of change in the field of transportation seems like a crawl, though, when compared to changes in the communications industry. Just a hundred years ago, the telegraph was our fastest message delivery system. Telephones, fax machines, television, radio, cellular phones and the computer have reduced the telegraph to a kind of communication camel caravan.

Think of the changes that have taken place in the last 10 years in your field of work. If you're in any kind of business, you've probably seen the leaders of your organization divide your company into units where each unit has assumed continually increasing profit objectives for which the unit managers are accountable. Those units that contribute (read: generate the most money) are labeled "core businesses"; those that don't are shut down, sold off or forced to compete with outside suppliers who can respond faster and more effectively.

Staying Competitive

The need to respond faster and more effectively in order to survive in today's constantly changing market has created the recent interest in self-directed work teams. From the beginning of the industrial revolution in the 19th century until the growth of unions in the 20th, the people at the top of any organization made the decisions and gave what we now call middle management the directives they needed to implement those decisions. Middle management, in turn, told workers how to complete the tasks necessary to enact their leaders' decisions and keep their jobs.

After World War II, business leaders required management to wear a kinder, gentler face. Workers now had access to management in the sense that they could make suggestions; occasionally management would even ask workers for advice. But the decision-making authority still rested with those at the top.

This management system worked well enough as long as there was little or no competition. The United States, for example, didn't win World War II because it could manufacture *better* planes and tanks than Germany or Japan; it won because it could produce *more* tanks and planes than all the warring countries combined. After the war, the United States found itself in the enviable position of being the wealthiest and most powerful country in world history. We lent money to our impoverished allies and defeated enemies so they could buy our products to help revive their economies and earn enough money to pay back their loans and buy more American products.

Unfortunately for Uncle Sam, Japanese and German leaders quickly realized that they couldn't compete any more effectively with cars and television sets than they had with tanks and planes. So what did they do? They created niches for themselves within the larger industrial markets. They created smaller, more fuel-efficient cars; they made television sets with better-quality sound and sharper pictures. Tactics of this sort taken alone, though, wouldn't have been enough to damage America's industrial might. They had to be combined with a new kind of management system: the self-directed work team.

The Self-Directed Work Team

Under this kind of system, much of the decision-making authority traditionally in the hands of those running an organization is given to teams made up of people who do the actual work. Employees no longer have to rely on directives or make suggestions and then wait for management to form a committee, conduct a study, reach a conclusion, make a decision, and implement a policy while the competition leaves them in the dust.

By placing decision-making authority in the hands of the teams, companies are able to respond faster to changes in the market. At 3M, for example, self-directed management teams have reduced from three years to 18 months the time it takes an idea to become a product. American companies that have instituted the Japanese and German work-team model — which, ironically, was invented by an American — have also discovered that people prefer to work on teams where they have a say rather than in traditional power structures where they're allowed to make suggestions but ultimately end up doing what they're told to do anyway. And, as a part of the decision-making process, team members find themselves more committed to the success of projects because the major decisions are theirs. They're also more willing to take greater risks because the responsibility for any outcome is shared by all the members of the team. In addition, team members learn they can accomplish more through a group than they can on their own, that new ideas are not necessarily wrong or inferior because they're different, that flexible people working interdependently can think of more solutions and more reasons why their solutions won't work than any single manager, that self-managed work teams can innovate faster and respond more rapidly than people working in a traditional power hierarchy, and that teams create leaders at all levels of organization.

In spite of the proven success of self-managed work teams, however, resistance to the team concept still comes from two main sources: those who have power and don't want to share it, and those who don't want power because they fear the responsibility that comes with it. What's going to happen to these people as businesses become more team-oriented and employees are required to take on increasingly greater shares of responsibility? The answer is obvious.

Not so obvious is why people hold onto traditional ways of doing things even when they know these ways are no longer effective and no longer in their best interests. In matters of change, people generally fall into three categories: those who love change because they've learned to benefit from it, those who refuse to change and are forced off the road of progress, and those who are uncomfortable with change but do what they have to do to survive. More than 80 percent of us fall into this third category.

In the Beginning....

Why? Because of our parents, of course. At least that's where our first ideas of power come from. Our first bosses, like it or not, were our parents. From birth we accepted their leadership because we were totally dependent on them. They trained us—sometimes more successfully than others—to do what they told us to do because they were our parents. As we grew older, we discovered ways to influence them, but they still had the final say in everything that was important.

When we started school, we experienced a similar paradigm; only this time our teachers were our bosses. If we attended a church, mosque or temple, a similar power hierarchy was run by rabbis, ministers, priests or mufti. The military—if we should have been so lucky—replaced parents, teachers and religious leaders with officers; business and industrial organizations substituted foremen, managers and supervisors. In other words, the playing field changed as we grew older, but our position on the team—be it at home, in school, at church, in the military or on the job — remained the same. In each power paradigm, we experienced increased shares of responsibility without corresponding increases in decision-making authority.

The result is that many of us had a very hard time growing up. Treated like adolescents in practically every organization in which we shared membership, the level of maturity required to carry on adult relationships with spouses, colleagues, and especially with those in authority, has not been easy to reach. Most people don't even know where it is, let alone how to get there. Like so many citizens in a nation of arrested adolescents, the great majority of today's workers go to their offices or plants with the same enthusiasm they reserved as teenagers for cleaning a room or mowing the lawn. And like many teenagers, their behavior is often unpredictable. One day they act like adults; the next day they behave worse than when they were children. How many times have you heard of an otherwise good employee respond to a new task with "That's not my job"?

And this situation is not likely to improve. In fact, it's getting much worse. In 1950, the *New York Times* conducted a survey in which thousands of teachers from all over the United States were asked to cite their three most pressing problems in the classroom. Their response? In order of severity: talking in class, cutting in line and chewing gum. The same survey was repeated in 1993. And the result this time? Violent crime, teenage pregnancy, teen suicide. Children no longer obey their parents and teachers just because they're their parents and teachers; a larger percentage of people leave the military than when there was a peacetime draft; religious institutions are made up mostly of senior citizens, and businesses can no longer rely on the loyalty of their employees. In short, the old authoritative way of running organizations is no longer effective.

Changing the Rules of Leadership

In his book *The Natural Superiority of Women*, Ashley Montague examines some of the theories as to why women live longer than men. One of his hypotheses, and a prediction for the future as well, argues that men have historically operated from positions of power.

Might, be it physical, technical, organizational or personal, was right. Women, on the other hand, have traditionally operated from positions of little or no power. As a result, they developed and learned to rely on a different set of skills: caring, listening, understanding, empathizing, negotiating, creating, communications.

If Montague is right—and current trends tend to indicate that he is—the skills traditionally associated with women are becoming increasingly more valued and rewarded. As the power once held by those at the top is relinquished or seized by those in the middle and at the bottom of traditional power hierarchies, the demand for people who can resolve conflicts, improve relationships and nurture others to realize their human potential continues to increase.

The creation of self-directed work teams is one extent to which business and industry are responding to the cultural and economic changes that have taken place in this country since World War II. Before World War I, corporations tried to keep workers dependent on them through, among other things, low wages and factory-owned stores and houses. With the rise of unions, corporate and industrial leaders began looking for signs of independence in the people they chose to succeed them, people who could make decisions, take risks and accept responsibility. Those whose only demonstrated abilities were to complete tasks and follow orders were no longer as highly valued.

Today's organizations still value independence but, through systems such as the self-managed work team, they are also searching for a higher level of maturity in their prospective leaders, namely, the ability to be *interdependent*. To survive in the new—and it is no longer a future—workplace, you need to specialize in your field but, at the same time, be flexible enough to learn new jobs and adapt quickly to sudden and continual changes in the economy. You also need to build relationships with clients, colleagues and customers that are based on mutual trust, rapport and credibility.

Enter the Enneagram

The Enneagram will help you in both areas by first of all providing you with the keys you need to know and understand yourself. Secure in the knowledge of who you are, you will have a clearer idea of what you want in your personal and professional life. You will also be better able to make the career choices that are most beneficial to your well-being and to that of those you love. This self-knowledge is also the first step toward knowing and understanding others.

The organizing principle of the Enneagram is simple, but it is by no means another self-help tool from the grab bag of pop psychology. Unlike traditional personality profiles that, since the time of Hippocrates, divide all human behaviors into four categories, the Enneagram spreads its personality characteristics over nine. Nor, like other behavior profiles, does it merely define and advise on how to respond to the various personalities. It also provides the paths we must follow to achieve increasingly greater levels of self-understanding and knowledge of the nature that identifies us as adult human beings. The insights it provides can run from the general to the particular and yet, as complex as the Enneagram is, its revelations are remarkably easy to understand and adopt.

But increasing self-knowledge and developing a greater understanding of others is not enough to make our lives at home fulfilling or our roles in the workplace more successful. We need to act on the wisdom we've gained, follow the specific steps required to prevent personal and professional crises in the future, bring to our daily tasks a newly acquired sense of vision and integrity, and concentrate on the changes we can control. In other words, the Enneagram isn't a onetime thing. It continually measures our commitment to what we believe in and what we know to be true.

Chapter 2
How to Use the Enneagram

No one knows when the Enneagram was invented. Some historians trace its origins to Babylon in BC 2500; all agree that it was used by Sufis in the 10th century. The Greeks named it—*ennea* means "nine"—sometime before the 14th century; the Spanish brought it to Bolivia and, during the 1960's and 1970's, the Jesuits cultivated its use in this country. Use of the Enneagram continues to proliferate for one simple reason: It works.

The most accurate and practical system available for understanding yourself and others, the Enneagram is a circle divided into three main parts, or groupings:

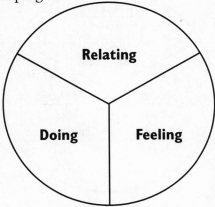

Nevertheless, the Enneagram does not pigeonhole everyone into one or another of these parts. It recognizes that we are all part Feelers, part Doers, and part Relaters. At the same time, we tend to exhibit the characteristics presented in one of the groupings more than we exhibit those of the other two. In other words, each one of us is *predominantly* a Feeler, a Doer or a Relater.

But each of these three groupings is too broad in scope and definition to do justice to the great variety we find in human behavior. For this reason, Enneagramists have subdivided each major group into three specifically defined personality types. **Feelers** are comprised of the Helper, the Entertainer and the Artist; **Doers** are separated into the Activist, the Disciple and the Thinker; **Relaters** are made up of the Driver, the Arbitrator and the Perfectionist.

Don't try to keep all these personality types in mind as you read this chapter. They will become familiar to you once you start using the Enneagram. Also, don't be discouraged if you didn't recognize yourself in any part of the circle yet. You will, once you read the definitions of the personality types. And, just to make sure you come up with a clear fix on where you fit, we've provided an evaluation for you to complete in Chapter 3. Your evaluation will not only identify your personality grouping, but will also identify your type within that grouping. For now, though, look at the Enneagram as we've described it.

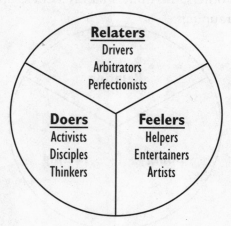

In the same way that we are all part Relaters, Feelers and Doers but predominate in only one of the major groupings, so too do we exhibit the behavior characteristics of each subgroup but predominate in only one. In other words, if you are predominantly a Feeler, you are also predominantly a Helper, an Entertainer or an Artist.

Each of the subgroups, as you might imagine, have both positive and negative characteristics that result in their placement in one of the three major groupings. Helpers, for example, have strengths and weaknesses that involve their Feelings; Perfectionists have strengths and weaknesses that have to do with their ability to Relate. And so on.

How each subgroup corresponds to its particular major grouping is seen by the position each subgroup is given within its grouping. One subgroup characteristic will overdevelop the character trait in its triad, a second subgroup will underdevelop its character trait, and a third will simply be out of touch with what makes it a part of a particular triad. Read on. You won't stay confused for long.

Let's look at just the Feeling triad for an example of what we're talking about.

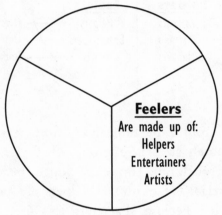

The first type listed here is the one that has overdeveloped the characteristic of the triad into which it has been placed. So Helpers are people who have overdeveloped their Feeling characteristics. Entertainers — the subgroup that's placed between Helpers and Artists — are most out of touch with their Feeling characteristics. Artists, then, are people who have underdeveloped their Feeling characteristics.

If this sounds like information overload, be patient. Like any other skill — think of swinging a tennis racquet or skiing down a hill — learning the Enneagram takes some time and practice. And like tennis or skiing, most of the learning will take place by doing rather than by reading. The purpose of this chapter is to familiarize you with the basic principles you want to have in mind before you explore in detail the different personality types.

If we look at the three major groupings and assign to them the dialectic associated with each subgroup, our Enneagram will look like this:

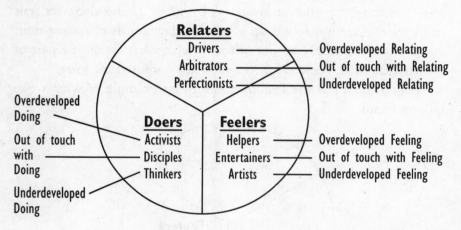

As we move around the Enneagram from segment to segment and look more closely at each subgroup, what we mean by "overdeveloped," "out of touch" and "underdeveloped" becomes more clear. In the Feeling triad, for example, Helpers are people who have overdeveloped their Feeling characteristics. They express most of their positive emotions and repress most of their negative ones. Because Entertainers project an image to substitute for who they really are, they are most out of touch with their Feelings. Artists are said to have underdeveloped any personal expression of their Feelings so they channel their emotions into some art form or form of aesthetic living.

The pattern we've just described in the Feeling triad is repeated in the Doing triad. The Thinker's ability to Do is underdeveloped, so Thinkers rarely get anything done. They're too busy wrestling with their increasingly complex and consequently isolated thoughts. Disciples, those out of touch with their Doer faculties, often can't act without the approval of some higher authority. Activists, as might be expected, have overdeveloped their ability to act; they are often hyperactive, sometimes even manic.

In the Relater triad, Drivers have overdeveloped their ability to relate to their environment; they see themselves as more important than anyone or anything else. Because Arbitrators are out of touch with their ability to relate to their environment as individuals, they identify with others and relate through them. Perfectionists under-develop their ability to relate to their environments, so nothing they do is ever good enough. They strive their whole lives to reach goals that will never satisfy them.

Because Enneagramists differ on the names they give each of the nine personality types — one person's "Disciple," for example, can be another person's "Loyalist" — they've assigned a number to each characteristic. These numbers remain constant no matter how wide-ly the names may vary. This is why we often hear Enneagramists identify themselves and others by their numbers, as in, "I'm a Two married to a Five."

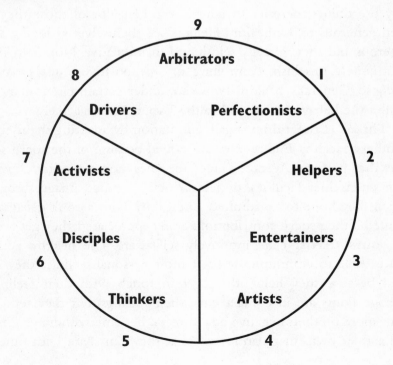

Now let's take a closer look at the positive and negative characteristics of each personality type. See if you can place yourself among the descriptions that follow. Don't be discouraged if you can't or if you choose more than one behavior type. These descriptions are admittedly broad and are presented here to give you a general idea of what we'll be discussing later in much greater detail.

Feelers

Be they Helpers, Entertainers or Artists, Feelers share characteristics relating to how they *feel* about themselves and others. Healthy, mature Feelers exhibit the positive characteristics of their personalities; unhealthy immature Feelers exhibit the negative ones.

Healthy Twos (Helpers), for example, are admired and appreciated for their ability to sustain positive and mature feelings for others. Kind, generous, understanding and able to empathize, they often go out of their way to help others without expecting anything in return. Average Twos are generous but, unlike their healthy cousins, they use their generosity to control the behavior of those they've been generous to. Unhealthy Helpers see themselves as loving and generous, but they're really selfish and manipulative. Note: No Two is *exclusively* unselfish, controlling or manipulative—just *predominantly* so. Generally healthy Twos can, under certain circumstances, exhibit the behavior of an unhealthy Two; it just isn't likely.

Threes (Entertainers) gain admiration by adapting themselves to others. Healthy Entertainers are valued because of the social services they perform. Average Threes, the ones most out of touch with their entertainer faculties, project a socially valued image through which they hope to be admired. Unhealthy Threes don't get disappointed if their social contributions aren't appreciated; they get even.

Fours (Artists) are intuitively self-aware. The healthy Fours, that is. Able to communicate their most personal feelings, they are liked because they help others get in touch with their feelings. Average Fours are in contact with their feelings, but they tend to focus more on their negative qualities and become withdrawn. They prefer their own imaginations to what they can share with others.

Unhealthy Fours are so negative about the way they feel about themselves, they become self-hating and possibly suicidal.

Twos, Threes and Fours (Helpers, Entertainers and Artists) are called Feelers because their assets and liabilities center on their feelings. When these types develop in mature ways, their feelings are the focus of what is admirable about them. Conversely, their feelings are the source of most of their problems. Those who perceive that they cannot be loved and appreciated for their own sakes develop a broad spectrum of strategies to earn respect and appreciation from others. These troubled, unhealthy Feelers have lost or given up what is true to their nature to match images that they believe are socially admirable. For this reason, the Feeling triad is also known as the Image triad; its central problem is *identity*. To confirm their self-images, Helpers (Twos) make themselves indispensable to others; Entertainers (Threes) direct their energies to building social images, and Artists (Fours) turn to art to report to the world what they've learned from their own self-absorption. When these Helpers, Entertainers and Artists are frustrated in their respective attempts to identify and communicate their feelings, they often resort to hostility toward others or, in the case of the many Artists, toward themselves.

Doers

Thinkers (Fives), Disciples (Sixes) and Activists (Sevens) share characteristics relating to their ability to get things done. Healthy Doers are known for their outstanding achievements; unhealthy Doers range from those who can't complete tasks to those whose accomplishments are frequently counterproductive to those whose behavior is completely out of control. Every achiever from the genius to the madman falls into this triad.

Fives (Thinkers) are analyzers. Healthy Fives, those capable of turning their brilliant thoughts into action, are valued for their ability to solve problems. Average Fives have great ideas, but they're so concerned with making sure their ideas are correct they rarely get around to acting on them. In other words: paralysis by analysis.

Unhealthy Twos think so much and become so isolated as a result of their thinking, they have a hard time distinguishing what is real from what is not.

Sixes (Disciples) benefit everyone when they are healthy. Loyal and committed, they can almost always be depended upon. Average Fives can be depended upon for their loyalty and commitment, but they won't act unless they secure some kind of permission from either a person in authority or an authoritative belief system. When they do act, average Sixes are often in rebellion to prove to themselves they are independent of the very authority they identify themselves with. Unhealthy Sixes are so dependent on authority, they feel inferior. Self-hating, self-humiliating and self-destructive, they often bring about the very failures they most want to avoid.

Sevens (Activists) are very busy; no day is long enough for them. Healthy Sevens accomplish many things in many fields; average Sevens do many things but are satisfied by only a few of them; unhealthy Sevens busily spin their wheels in a frenzy of hyperactivity.

In the same way that Feelers focus much of their time and energy on image, so too can Doers become overly concerned with *insecurity*. Often their search for what is safe leads them to withdraw into an intellectual world they can control. Or they pin their hopes for security on an authoritative figure or institution. By always doing what they're told, these Doers never have to be responsible for the ways they behave. Other Doers never stop doing. By constantly engaging in some activity or other, they achieve security by never having time to face the fear of insecurity.

Relaters

Drivers (Eights), Arbitrators (Nines) and Perfectionists (Ones) are concerned with how they relate to their environments. Eights want to dominate it, Nines want to coexist with it and Ones want to perfect it.

The secret of success for healthy **Eights (Drivers)** centers on their ability to see themselves as better than everyone else. Confident and accomplished, they inspire confidence in others and lead them to accomplishments they might not have reached on their own. Average Eights achieve, but, rather than lead others, they step all over them on their way to the top, which they don't often reach because of the avenging enemies they made along the way. Unhealthy Eights make sure they make it to the top by destroying anyone who gets in their way, thereby preventing any possibilities for revenge.

Healthy Nines (Arbitrators) know how to identify, sympathize and empathize. Through their ability to accept and understand, they make people feel comfortable and assured, thereby providing for them a base from which they can grow. Average Nines undermine themselves and others by idealizing the people they relate to. By placing others, be they persons or ideas, on pedestals, average Nines create an image that can't possibly be lived up to. Unhealthy Nines hold onto their false illusions to the point that they often alienate themselves from reality.

Ones (Perfectionists) are the most objective in this triad. Reasonable, logical and fair, they win friends and influence people by their clear understanding of issues and their innate ability to distinguish right from wrong. Average Ones, however, allow their emotions to get in the way of their ability to be objective. As a result, they try to force their environments into a state of absolute perfection. Because everything in their lives can be improved, even the excellent cannot satisfy them. Unhealthy Ones become so obsessed with the deficiencies in others, they fail to see their own weaknesses and shortcomings.

The principal problem facing Relaters is *frustration* with an imperfect world. For them, strength, self-assertion and determination are vital for sustaining their self-images. Nines (Arbitrators) can turn their anger against themselves or distance themselves from feeling anger. In this latter situation, Nines see even normal assertive behavior as aggressive. Ones (Perfectionists) can also be hard on themselves, but their mastery of the "should" and "must" isn't limited to their own imperfections. With their blindingly clear sense of right and wrong, they can be cruel toward others.

Having read these brief descriptions of the nine personality types that make up the Enneagram, you may have been able to place yourself in one of the triads (Feeling, Doing, Relating) but not in one of the specific categories. Or perhaps you see yourself in several subgroups but not limited to a particular major group. Either experience may be a natural response to what is negative in the various types. To test the veracity of this response, ask yourself what type the people who know you best would assign you. Or ask yourself what upsets you the most about each of the types that is closest to describing your personality.

One of the goals of the Enneagram is to make you aware of the changes you need to make to become a mature, more fully developed human being. To succeed you must be willing to address the unpleasant truths about yourself, to rid yourself of the limiting behavior that keeps you from becoming the person you're capable of being, and to work hard to handle the changes that mature, emotional growth requires. The individual chapters on each personality type will tell you how.

In addition to providing a map upon which you can trace and measure your emotional growth, the Enneagram also traces the paths that lead to deterioration and neurosis. This is what we mean when we say the Enneagram is "dynamic" or "open-ended." No one is "stuck" in any single category; everyone is given a path leading to mature behavior and one leading to immature behavior.

You've already noted that the numbers on the Enneagram are connected in a specific sequence: One through Nine. But the numbers are also connected in another way: by lines. These lines indicate whether you are moving positively or negatively from your basic personality type.

This next representation of the Enneagram depicts its positive directions: 1→7→5→8→2→4→1. This means that a One (the Perfectionist) who already exhibits highly mature traits wants to begin taking on the mature traits associated with type Seven (the Activist). A mature Seven, in turn, wants to move in the direction of a Five (Thinker). And so on.

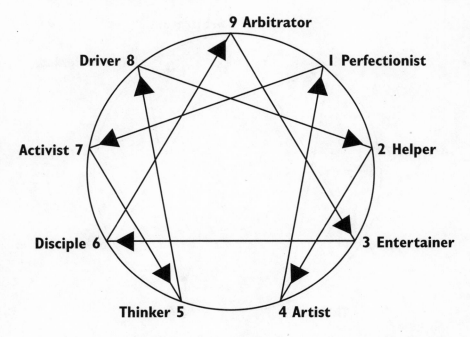

Conversely, the Enneagram's next representation indicates its negative directions: 1→4→2→8→5→7→1. In this sequence, a One (the Perfectionist) who exhibits immature traits wants to learn to recognize and avoid the unhealthy characteristics of a Four (the Artist). A Four, in turn, wants to move away from the immaturity exhibited by a Two (the Helper).

A Four who successfully avoids deteriorating into a Two and manages to reach the level of a healthy One, however, does not stop growing at One. Rather, the newly arrived One wants to work on the positive traits in this category, master them as best as he or she can, and then move on to the next level of maturity. In the case of a One, the next level of mature emotional growth is a healthy Seven.

Now we see how the Enneagram goes beyond the static characterization of traditional personality categories. Its representation outlines the psychological processes for becoming more mature or immature human beings. Take, for example, a Six (the Disciple). A Six who exhibits mature traits is already cultivating the seeds he or she will need to acquire the mature traits of a Nine (the Arbitrator).

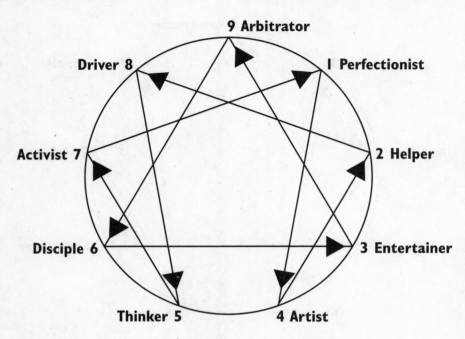

The principle problem for Sixes, however, is insecurity. Fearing risks, they often need permission from some authority before trying anything new. If they can take the risks necessary to move to the next level — and healthy Sixes are in the best position to do this — they will become less anxious and more confident as their independent actions generate success. A Six who exhibits immature traits, however, runs the risk of slipping into the immature behavior of a Three (the Entertainer). Whereas the immature Six was merely anxiety-ridden, suspicious and perhaps paranoid, the Six who is taking on the characteristics of a Three strikes out at those who threaten him or her. Your goal, then, is to locate your type on the Enneagram, develop the positive characteristics of that type, and move on to the healthy traits associated with the next level of maturity. There you want to repeat the process and move on again until you've acquired the best qualities of all nine personality types.

Before identifying or confirming what you believe to be your personalty type through the Mattone Enneagram Inventory, however, you need to keep in mind one more thing:

The Success of the Enneagram Depends on You.

This means, first of all, having the Right Attitude. Without the Right Attitude, you can apply all the lessons of the Enneagram and never come off as being more than a phony, a fool and a failure. So, what attitude do you need to make your newfound skills work?

- **Be yourself.** Trying to conform to the images of others — be they husbands, wives, relatives, friends, colleagues or bosses — is to become mentally anorexic. While you shrink into a mere skeleton of what you could be, all you can see is the psychological fat you've been conditioned to attack yourself with. No one has to see your Mattone Enneagram Inventory results but you; no one but you has to know where you are on the Enneagram or in what direction you are heading.

- **Forget about the past.** Repeat what worked well, improve upon your mistakes, and move on. If you want to *understand* why you behaved the ways you did, change your behavior and then compare the differences brought about by the change.

- **Imagine the ideal you.** *You* is the key word here, not someone else's idea of who you should be. In other words, stop "shoulding" on yourself. Use the Enneagram to create a picture of yourself at the levels of maturity that you want to reach.

- **Think, look and act the part.** If your image of yourself is a healthy Five (the Thinker) on your way to becoming a mature Eight (the Driver), think of yourself as a healthy Five. You may not be the most healthy Five in the whole world — there can be only one of those — but you can be among the healthy ones. Now ask yourself: How does a healthy Five look and behave in the presence of friends, relatives, colleagues, clients and bosses? Got the picture? Now follow in your behavior the blueprint you created in your mind.

- **Don't compare yourself to others.** The Enneagram is not a competition. Each personality is different, and each has something to contribute. Focus instead on what you do well, discover how you can do it better, and use the Enneagram to help you improve in areas where your behavior isn't what you want it to be.

- **Reward your accomplishments.** It doesn't matter how small they may be. Lack of closure and lack of celebration are major causes of stress. So take some time to enjoy what you've done and treat yourself to something special: a dinner out, a movie, some extra time with your family or friends.

- **Don't be afraid.** Fear is not a sign of failure: It's a sign of fear. It's not a behavior: It's an emotion. So accept it—you probably have good reasons to be afraid of change. As a matter of fact, a little fear will often go a long way toward helping you succeed. Ask yourself, "What's the worst thing that could happen?" If that happened, what would you do? Because the worst probably won't happen, how would you handle the next worst thing? Instead of looking at every disaster from your present point of view, look at it as if it's already taken place. By starting at the worst outcome and working backward, you can anticipate disasters and make plans to avoid them. Being emotionally mature doesn't mean you're never afraid, never get nervous, or occasionally think you will fail. Being emotionally mature, regardless of your personality type, means having the confidence to accept who you are while working to make yourself better.

Having the Right Attitude won't ensure that the Enneagram will automatically turn you into an emotionally mature human being, but having the Wrong Attitude almost guarantees your emotional deterioration. Having the Right Attitude, then, also means taking the Right Action.

Right Action people take fate into their own hands; they don't allow circumstances to dictate their behavior. Right Action people bring to their lives a vision of who they are and who they want to be. They approach each step on the road to maturity with a sense of integrity, honesty and responsibility for their behavior. Right Action people concentrate on what they can control; they don't create anxiety for themselves by worrying about things they can do nothing about. Finally, Right Action people do things right; they take the risks necessary to satisfy themselves and those they care about. Wrong Action people play by the book, follow the rules and make no exceptions for anyone. Not even themselves.

To become a Right Action user of the Enneagram:

- **Focus on what you can control.** Worrying about anything else will only lead to frustration, disappointment, depression and failure.
- **Be willing to take risks.** Success isn't possible without them.
- **Be patient.** You can't overcome all your bad habits in the time it takes you to identify them and plan what you want to change in your life. But you can start to overcome your bad habits in the time it takes you to create that plan.
- **Have a sense of humor.** Don't take yourself too seriously; there's no situation in life that can't be overcome with humor.
- **Don't give up.** Setbacks aren't failures: they're setbacks.
- **Repeat what works.** This also applies to what you see others doing that works. If you see them behaving in ways you admire, emulate their behavior until it becomes your own.

Being Right Active and following your own Enneagram map is a lifelong process. The personality type that best identifies you is not as important as what you do about it.

Chapter 3
The Mattone
Enneagram Inventory

This may take some time, but the results will be well worth your time and effort. As you might imagine, each statement in the Mattone Enneagram Inventory corresponds to one of the Enneagram's nine personality types. The first scoring sheet in this section, for example, lists the questions that correspond to the behavior most frequently experienced by people with Helper characteristics. The following page lists the numbers of the statements pertaining to Entertainers. And so on.

Your task is to record your response (1, 2, 3, 4 or 5) on the line following each statement. When you're done filling in your response numbers, add them up and record the sum in the score box at the bottom of each Personality page.

Do this for each personality type even if you believe you already know your type. You may be surprised, especially if you're certain you're not a 3 (Entertainer), a 6 (Disciple) or a 9 (Arbitrator).

Scoring Sheet for Type Two

The Helper

Statement: Your Score

I prefer working to help people on a one-to-one basis
as opposed to a team basis.   _____

I think I am more people-oriented than goal-oriented.   _____

I am less disciplined; I know how to be spontaneous
and improvise.   _____

Sometimes I am gripped by a feeling of amazement
and gratitude for what I have in my life   _____

I spend my time with the interpersonal and emotional
(as opposed to the abstract and mental) aspects of the
people and situations I encounter.   _____

I find I often get attached to people.   _____

I often sense what's going on inside others before they
say it out loud.   _____

I like to use the telephone and make lots of calls.   _____

I don't like to admit it, but I get into other people's
business more than I should.   _____

I feel good about having other people depend on me.   _____

A lot of thankless tasks fall on my shoulders. I wish
others would think of me for a change.   _____

I am often not sure whether the affection other people
have for me is sincere or if they like me just because
I'm nice to them.   _____

Your Total Score [   ]

5=Strongly Agree; 4=Agree; 3=Partially Agree/Disagree; 2=Disagree; 1=Strongly Disagree

Scoring Sheet for Type Three

The Entertainer

Statement:	Your Score
My business associates would describe me as diplomatic, charming and ambitious.	_____
I think I am more goal-oriented than people-oriented.	_____
I am ambitious and push myself to realize my dreams.	_____
I know how to motivate people and awaken their enthusiasm.	_____
It's important to me to let others know how I feel, although I may express myself indirectly.	_____
I find I often get competitive with my business associates.	_____
It's important to me to make favorable impressions.	_____
I enjoy getting attention from others and being in the limelight.	_____
Typically when I get angry, I become distant and icy.	_____
I enjoy talking about myself and being the center of attention.	_____
It really bothers me when others don't think favorably about me.	_____
For the sake of my career, I am prepared to neglect my family, friends and marriage.	_____

Your Total Score [   ]

5=Strongly Agree; 4=Agree; 3=Partially Agree/Disagree; 2=Disagree; 1=Strongly Disagree

Scoring Sheet for Type Four

The Artist

Statement: Your Score

One of my greatest assets that I bring to the
workplace is the depth of my feelings.   _____

It's important to me to let others know how I feel,
although I may express myself indirectly.   _____

I don't mind revealing my weaknesses to others, and
often do.   _____

Life is like a drama in which I am both actor
and spectator.   _____

I am not all that practical and somewhat of a dreamer.   _____

When I get angry at others, I find it difficult to
confront them.   _____

I have the feeling that I can never be completely
fulfilled.   _____

I have always dreamed of becoming a painter, poet,
singer or something like that.   _____

I feel uneasy talking about myself and being the
center of attention.   _____

I feel uncomfortable when people depend on me.   _____

I sometimes hold myself back too much and am
blocked from doing good things for myself.   _____

Deep down, I don't really feel "at home" anywhere.   _____

Your Total Score [   ]

5=Strongly Agree; 4=Agree; 3=Partially Agree/Disagree; 2=Disagree; 1=Strongly Disagree

Scoring Sheet for Type Five

The Thinker

Statement:	Your Score
One of my greatest assets is the sharpness of my mind.	_____
People come to me because I have the knowledge that they need.	_____
I like to browse in bookstores and libraries.	_____
It's important to me to see things as objectively as possible.	_____
I tend to be unconventional and idiosyncratic at work.	_____
I hesitate to act until I have thought things through carefully.	_____
I need my own study time or at least my own corner to withdraw to when everything gets overwhelming.	_____
I like to be alone.	_____
I know if I have done something well, and I don't need the reactions of others to confirm it.	_____
I distrust authority and ignore rules as much as possible.	_____
People have said that I am argumentative—I guess I enjoy a good debate.	_____
I often don't put my good ideas down on paper, and projects that I have in my head often stay in the planning stage.	_____

Your Total Score ☐

5=Strongly Agree; 4=Agree; 3=Partially Agree/Disagree; 2=Disagree; 1=Strongly Disagree

Scoring Sheet for Type Six

The Disciple

Statement: Your Score

I prefer working with others in a team effort.   _____

I am practical and down to earth.   _____

I am well disciplined, organized, and I know how to
follow through on details.   _____

For me it's important to be proactive about the
future so I'll be better prepared to handle whatever
comes my way.   _____

When I am unsure of what to do on a project,
I get advice from others.   _____

I tend to be a "regular" kind of person; a traditionalist
in the truest sense of the word.   _____

I like to work within the framework of an organization.   _____

There is a little bit of storyteller and entertainer in me.   _____

It makes me furious when others don't follow policies
and procedures and they get away with it.   _____

It's difficult for me not to complain when others
don't do their jobs and put me under more pressure.   _____

One of my fears is being taken advantage of.   _____

I have the impression that so called "authorities"
are incompetent, but I usually hesitate to take action
against them.   _____

Your Total Score _____

5=Strongly Agree; 4=Agree; 3=Partially Agree/Disagree; 2=Disagree; 1=Strongly Disagree

Scoring Sheet for Type Seven

The Activist

Statement:	Your Score
I am like the weather: I change constantly.	_____
I like to try many different things and am eager for new work experiences.	_____
There is a little bit of storyteller and entertainer in me.	_____
When my job gives me lemons, I make lemonade.	_____
When I need to make a decision, I try different things to see what works best.	_____
It's important for me that something always is "going on."	_____
Other people say I talk fast.	_____
I like to engage others in verbal duels with quick and humorous repartee.	_____
It is hard for me not to put down others who can't keep pace with me.	_____
I like "letting go" and pushing the limits.	_____
When projects or relationships get too boring, I abandon them.	_____
Fairly often, I treat myself to things that are actually too expensive for me.	_____

Your Total Score [　　　]

5=Strongly Agree; 4=Agree; 3=Partially Agree/Disagree; 2=Disagree; 1=Strongly Disagree

Scoring Sheet for Type Eight

The Driver

Statement: Your Score

I act quickly, confident that I can work things out
if things have gone awry.   _____

I am like a rock; steady and sure.   _____

I persuade people with my confidence and the
strength of my personality.   _____

I have always been concerned about justice and
what is "right" at work.   _____

One of my fears is being dependent on someone else.   _____

"Winning" is critical to me in everything that I do.   _____

I like to call the shots at work.   _____

I like to negotiate and make deals.   _____

When I get angry, I tell people off.   _____

I don't fear having conflicts with others.   _____

I don't care if others like me as long as they respect me. _____

I don't want to reveal my weaknesses to others and
rarely do.   _____

Your Total Score [   ]

5=Strongly Agree;   4=Agree;   3=Partially Agree/Disagree;   2=Disagree;   1=Strongly Disagree

Scoring Sheet for Type Nine

The Arbitrator

Statement: Your Score

People confide in me because I make them feel
safe and appreciated.   _____

I am an optimist at work.   _____

I value having a good atmosphere at work.   _____

Sometimes I am gripped by a feeling of amazement
and gratitude for what I have in my life.   _____

I am not very ambitious for myself, but I work
hard for my loved ones.   _____

It's not always important to me to tell others how
I feel.·   _____

I don't handle pressure well at work and I work
best at my own pace.   _____

I realize that I sometimes avoid thinking about
my problems.   _____

I don't like to admit it, but I let little problems go
until they become big problems.   _____

People say I'm too accommodating.   _____

I fear having conflicts with others.   _____

I let things run their course—problems often take
care of themselves.   _____

Your Total Score [   ]

5=Strongly Agree;   4=Agree;   3=Partially Agree/Disagree;   2=Disagree;   1=Strongly Disagree

Scoring Sheet for Type One

The Perfectionist

Statement: Your Score

People describe me as formal, direct and mature.   _____

I persuade people with my honesty and the
reasonableness of my agruments.   _____

I am a teacher and a coach.   _____

I am prepared to put up with disadvantages rather
than sacrificing personal standards.   _____

I don't like being critical, but I can't help noticing
when things are wrong.   _____

I put my ideals over obtaining "practical results."   _____

In my work, everything has to have its place.   _____

I am often under time pressure.   _____

I don't like losing control of myself when things
get tough at work.   _____

In my thoughts I often criticize myself.   _____

I often feel muscular tension (neck, shoulders, etc.).   _____

Others often feel criticized by me.   _____

Your Total Score ☐

5=Strongly Agree; 4=Agree; 3=Partially Agree/Disagree; 2=Disagree; 1=Strongly Disagree

Profile Instructions

Having totaled your responses on each of the pages identifying a specific personality type, transfer those scores to the corresponding boxes on the Mattone Enneagram Profile on the next page spread. Then come back and finish reading this page.

Your highest score indicates your *basic personality type* at work. The mean score for each type is 36. If your personality were in perfect balance, you would score 36 on each of the nine types. This result, as you might imagine, is very rare. A wide range of variations from the mean with some scores falling above the mean and some below is much more typical. These variations produce a profile of your personality with the imbalances representing your ever-changing responses to work. The "overdeveloped" and "underdeveloped" ranges on the profile, therefore, are not to be interpreted as indications of psychological concern or value judgments. They only indicate the relative development of your overall maturity and versatility at work. If, for example, you score at or above the "overdeveloped" line on one or more of the types, those types are strong aspects of who you are, and you may wish to devote less attention to these characteristics and spend more time emphasizing those that are underdeveloped.

Note that the Mattone Enneagram Inventory and Profile are only the first steps toward knowing ourselves better. For this reason, the profile is not a conclusive "finding," but a snapshot that sheds light on how we see ourselves at work. Your basic personality type, by the way, never changes. What does change is your level of maturity. One of the purposes of the Enneagram is to provide the path each personality must follow to achieve full emotional maturity. With this in mind, you may wish to ask five associates — people with whom you work closely — to fill out the Mattone Enneagram Inventory with you in mind. Comparing your assessment with how others at work see you can provide a valuable insight into who you are and who you may want to be.

Mattone Enneagram Profile

TYPE	FEELERS		DOERS				RELATERS		
	Two	Three	Four	Five	Six	Seven	Eight	Nine	One
	The Helper	The Entertainer	The Artist	The Thinker	The Disciple	The Activist	The Driver	The Arbitrator	The Perfectionist
SCORE	☐	☐	☐	☐	☐	☐	☐	☐	☐

60
59
58
57
56
55
54
53
52
51
50
59
58
57
56
55
54 · overdeveloped
53
52
51
50
49
48
47

mean

underdeveloped

36

For a comprehensive, confidential written evaluation that details the strengths and weaknesses of your basic personality and offers suggestions for becoming increasingly more versatile and mature, send a copy of each of your scoring sheets along with a check in the amount of $250 to:

John Mattone
Mattone Enterprises
26 Grand Oak Road
Forestdale, MA 02644

PART II

FEELERS

Chapter 4

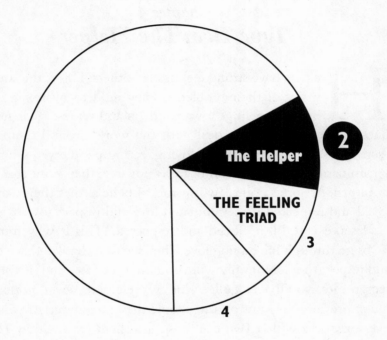

Your success and happiness lie in you...
Resolve to keep happy,
and your joy and you shall form
an invincible host against difficulties.
—Helen Keller

Chapter 4
Type Two: The Helper

H elpers have strong feelings for others. This is the source of many of their problems. They tend to overexpress their positive feelings toward others and repress their negative ones in their attempts to deal with the world around them. Their "sense of self" is that they are loving, caring people yet, when they act immaturely, their love and care is not free; they want something in return. At some point, Twos came to believe that they would be loved and respected if they initiated love and respect toward others: "If I serve you, I'll be loved and respected." This is why immature Twos go through life buying love. They see to it that you have to love and respect them. Not only will you have no choice, but if you don't reciprocate, you'll feel guilty. And yet Helpers never notice how much pressure they put on the people they care about. Anyone who lives or works with a Two can sense this silent expectation; Helpers are always looking for more attention, a bigger response.

Mature Twos are considerate and genuinely the most loving of all the personality types. Because they have strong feelings toward others, they often go out of their way to help people, doing real good and serving real needs. If they move toward immaturity, though, Twos become dishonest about the presence of their aggressive feelings. They consequently don't see themselves the same way others see them, namely, as manipulative. Immature Twos love and respect others — but "with strings attached." Even though they have a strong need to be loved and respected, they're careful not to make their need obvious. As a result, they often operate indirectly. Think of the kind of person who sends Christmas cards only to those on the list of people who returned the previous year's cards.

Because Helpers have a problem with *identity,* they often deny their aggressiveness toward others and frequently conceal their hostility even from themselves. In fact, the only time they act aggressively is when they've convinced themselves they're behaving for someone else's good. To admit their aggressiveness contradicts their self-created images and alienates the people they need. Helpers, therefore, deny their selfish or aggressive motives or interpret them as appropriate. As they perfect this mode of behavior, the distance between Helpers' motives and their behaviors becomes significant. One result is that they force others into dependent relationships controlled by the Helpers. This, in turn, infuriates the beloveds who know they're being controlled and feel forced to confirm "The Helper's" viewpoint of how virtuous they are. Interpersonal conflicts are inevitable with Twos, but what further complicates the difficulty is the Helpers' conviction that they always are "more sinned against than sinning." The major focus of Twos, then, is on themselves, although they neither give this impression to others nor think of themselves this way.

Mature Twos

Mature Twos are empathetic, caring, compassionate and full of feeling toward others. The Profile:

- Prefer close personal relationships
- Support and actively listen to others
- Are warm, accepting and friendly
- Work slowly and cohesively with others
- Are agreeable, steady, calm and supportive
- Share personal feelings
- Demonstrate good counseling skills
- Handle conflict well
- Encourage support from others
- Prefer first names to last
- Focus more on relationships than tasks
- Are generous, unselfish and love others with "no strings attached"

Average Twos

Average Twos tend to talk more about their own feelings than those of others. The Profile:

- Talk more about love than act on it
- Are emotionally demonstrative
- Give attention to others to the point of flattery
- Are intimate and solicitous to the point of hovering or meddling
- Interfere with others' lives under the guise of caring
- Try to control those they have "invested" in
- Want people to depend on them
- Want to be informed on everything
- Like to be sought out for advice
- Expect to be constantly thanked and honored for their goodness

Immature Twos

Immature Twos feel unappreciated. They:

- Become resentful and complain
- Disguise their motives behind friendly gestures
- Are manipulative and self-serving
- Try to make people feel guilty
- Undermine others by disparaging them
- Control to the point of domineering
- Feel entitled to get what they want
- Are disappointed when their favors aren't repaid
- Feel victimized and used
- Rationalize their response to people's ingratitude

To move toward increasingly greater levels of maturity, Helpers need to follow the sequence presented on the Enneagram as: 2→4→1→7→5→8.

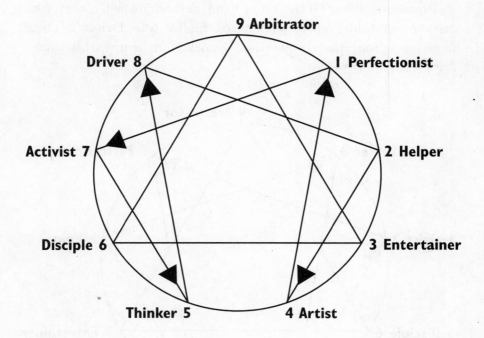

In other words, you move along the Enneagram as you become more mature and versatile. If you're already a mature Two, you want to take on the healthy attributes of a Four (the Artist). Mature Two's accept the presence of their negative feelings as completely as they accept their positive feelings. Because they have become emotionally honest, they are able to express their full range of emotions: happiness, fear, guilt, worry, sadness, etc. Instead of playing the conditional love and respect game, they have learned to accept themselves and others unconditionally. Love and respect are given to them not for what they do for others but for *who they are*. These Helpers have learned to be comfortable about revealing themselves; their relationships have become honest, human and reciprocal.

Immature Twos, on the other hand, deteriorate when they take ·on the unhealthy characteristics of Eights (the Drivers). Their negative progression on the Enneagram runs this way: 2→8→5→7→1→4.

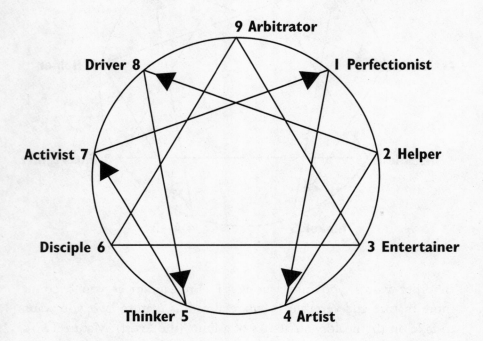

The major problem for immature Twos is that they have not come to grips with their aggressive feelings. They resent those who are ungrateful to them and are quick to strike out at those who have not responded to them the way they wanted. The hatred they have suppressed comes out and is openly expressed against those whom Twos feel have not loved them sufficiently in the past. This is the classic passive/aggressive type.

When Helpers talk to themselves, here are some things they say:

Basic Fear
"I fear being unloved and unwanted for myself/who I am. I fear that others will not love and respect me unless I make others love and respect me."

Basic Motivation
"I have a strong need to be loved and respected."

Mature Sense of Who I Am
"I am a giving, caring and loving person."

My Greatest Irritation
*"I work hard to love and respect others. I don't understand why
they don't love and respect me the same way in return."*

The Spark That Ignites My Movement Toward Defensiveness
*"I think that all my actions are done with good intent, that I
connect with others without condition and that there are no ulterior
motives that define my relationships with others."*

My Greatest Sin
*"I partake in goodness that calls attention to itself so that my
goodness will be admired. I want to be seen as good, humble, self-sacrificing
and hope that my generosity will be repaid.*

My Greatest Strength
*"I am charitable. When I'm mature, I love and respect others unconditionally.
I don't need thank yous. I help others for the sake of others."*

The Helper at Work

When they're mature, the Helper is most apt to have compatible
working relationships with others. They have patience, staying power
and are motivated to make relationships work. Helpers are generally
uncomfortable with conflict unless they're moving toward maturity.
They are vigilant about how others complete tasks but rarely say
anything negative about what they observe. Because they want love
and respect, Helpers don't make waves. Instead, they often shoulder
a major share of duties and won't say anything to their boss or their
fellow employees. When they're mature, Helpers can be great teachers, coaches or tutors because they are selfless in their need to help
others. Hence, they gravitate toward occupations where there is a
high level of interaction. Whether in group or one-on-one contact,
Helpers welcome the opportunity to support others.

Helpers seek inclusion and prefer to work in relationships on a casual, first-name basis. Mature Helpers seek more in-depth friendships with selected coworkers than the other personality types. But Helpers also want reciprocity in their relationships. If they contribute harmony to the work group, they expect something in return. Often they make others feel dependent on them or, because they need reciprocity, they can often cause conflicts.

Mature Helpers are great listeners and they expect others to listen as well. They like people who share their thoughts, feelings and experiences. Less mature Helpers, however, tend to be more indirect.

Strategies for Working With Helpers

Building rapport, trust and credibility with others often depends on how versatile we are. Versatility is also a measure of how others endorse us. Individuals who have learned to meet the demands of others in a wide variety of situations tend to be accepted by more people; individuals not as resourceful in meeting the varied interpersonal demands will be accepted by fewer people. The more versatile you are, then, the more capable you will be at coping effectively with change.

As you read this book and begin to practice the strategies for growing, maturing and becoming more versatile, learn to separate your reactions to people from their reactions to you. If, from their behavior, you can identify someone as a Helper, here are some tips for improving your relationship with them.

1. Take initiative to show you are interested in these people as people. Ask about what's important to them as individuals, then support these people in terms of their personal needs.

2. Mature Helpers want to work with you to achieve their personal objectives but, because their personal goals are often understated, you may have to work closely with them to learn the specifics of who, what, when, where, why and how. Be careful not to exaggerate the extent of your interest. If a Helper senses you are coming on too strong, the Helper will be disappointed

and believe he or she is shouldering most of the work.

3. Be patient and encourage the Helper to open up about unstated goals. Helpers tend to verbalize spontaneously about other people's goals because they want to find common ground. Therefore, it is critical that you get Helpers to articulate their own goals so you will be in a better position to satisfy their needs.

4. If you agree on an objective and begin to take action, check back early with your Helper to see if he or she disagrees or is unhappy with the way the project is developing. Encourage the Helper to anticipate and articulate potential areas of disagreement before they occur. Show your Helper how disagreements can be expressed in an open, honest and professional way. Helpers need to learn that respect and conflict are not synonymous. They can still be loved and respected as professionals, even though people disagree.

5. If you disagree, focus on the issue and not the personality of the Helper. At the same time, you want to solicit the Helper's personal input.

6. Because Helpers tend to be less disciplined about time, make sure they have enough for the completion of any project. Be patient and don't force them to make decisions too quickly. You may feel you know clearly what you'd like to achieve in working with the Helper and you may feel that you can get the Helper to respond quickly, but this can backfire later on, especially if the Helper perceives he or she didn't have a satisfactory opportunity to express an opinion or that things moved too quickly. If this happens, Helpers will resist your ideas. You will get more results from Helpers if you can move slowly, cautiously, casually and informally. Show the Helper that you are an agreeable type of person and that you are interested in him or her as a person.

7. Show that you care. If you are willing to listen and be responsive to your Helper's needs, you can discover the negative feelings. This is of great benefit to you because Helpers tend to overex-

press their positive feelings and underexpress the negative ones. Your candid openness and honesty will bring you what you really want to hear and can be highly motivational to your Helpers.

8. Be patient. Helpers use opinions (as opposed to facts) to avoid risks when making decisions, especially if a decision might upset relationships at work. If you have been successful supporting a Helper's feelings and you've spent time building honest agreements, influencing his or her decisions will not be difficult. The Helper wants your *personal guarantee* that the decision you are asking him or her to make is the correct one. Because of your friendship and acceptance, the Helper wants you to support and do what you can to back up the decision. Probably the quickest way to irritate a Helper is to provide personal assurances and then not honor your commitment. Therefore, it is vital that your guarantee or personal assurances be realistic and understood by the Helper as such.

Strategies for Helping the Helper in You

1. Ask yourself what your boss/employees/customers *need* and then help them attain it. Giving people what they need and not necessarily what they want or what you think will make them happy makes you truly helpful.

2. Let your quality service, your unselfishness and your goodness stand on their own merits. Be respectful of genuine talent and encourage real strengths. Be generous without attaching any "strings." If you are good, people will seek you out and respect you. You don't have to manipulate others into liking you.

3. Be more conscious of your need to be loved and the conditional games you play, as in "I love you; therefore you must love me." When you play this game, you pressure yourself and others to satisfy an agreement that exists only in your head.

4. Don't call attention to yourself and your efforts. After you have helped someone, let it go. Don't look for a return.

5. Don't fall into the habit of trying to get people to love you by giving them undeserved praise. Conversely, don't withdraw sup-

port from those you don't like. What you do for others should not be based solely on what they have or have not done for you.

6. Cultivate new relationships, but don't forget to honor your primary relationships (spouse, children, etc.).

7. Work behind the scenes more and don't advertise the good you do.

8. Try not to be possessive or controlling. Everybody deserves to have his or her own experiences.

9. Be sure your motives for helping others are pure and unselfish. Don't hide behind intentions you know are insincere; you will never be judged on intentions, only on your actions.

Chapter 5

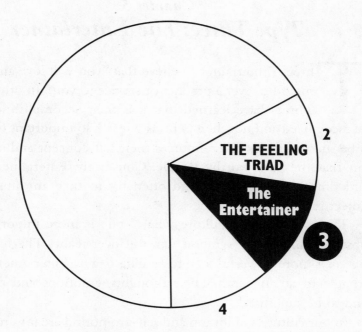

I studied the lives of great men and famous women;

and I found that the men and women who got to the top

were those who did the jobs they had in hand, with everything

they had of energy, enthusiasm and hard work.

—Harry Truman

Chapter 5
Type Three: The Entertainer

Threes (Entertainers) believe that "you will love and respect me if I deliver a product or service to you." In other words, Threes have learned that it is their accomplishments that are recognized and not them. This is why it's so important for Threes to be successful. Success reinforces their self-concept and belief system that they are worthy people. Conversely, Entertainers have a hard time handling failure and often try to turn any unsuccessful project into one more success.

Threes thrive in a culture where style is more important than substance, and where symbols win out over reality. The temptation to *seem* is more powerful than to *be*. This is why Entertainers have to struggle to attain depth. Their thoughts, emotions and demeanor tend to be superficial.

In our culture, exhibition and self-promotion are rewarded. They are even necessary to get noticed in the competitive marketplace. The goal, therefore, is to win. To be famous. To be recognized. The quest for success and prestige can hardly be escaped. The media tell us how to dress for success, how to eat for success, how to network for success and we, if we're not careful, make real the fantasy that our identities are determined by certain conventions. If these conventions are adhered to, we will become stars.

This is why Threes, unlike the Twos who tend to "overexpress their feelings," are most seriously "out of touch" with their emotional lives. Contact with their feelings is lost because their energy is directed toward building their social image. Entertainers fear identifying with their deeper feelings because they mistrust who they are. They believe they are only lovable and respected when they meet others' expectations. Because Threes have a fundamental problem with their identities, there is a major split between who they seem to be and who they are. In time, who they seem to be (their image) becomes their reality.

Mature Threes are admired because they have worked hard to acquire the qualities and skills they seem to embody. They have a strong self-concept and are recognized as outstanding people. Without Threes, a lot of good things would never happen. In fact, Threes get three times as much done as anyone else and probably 10 times as much as the Nine (The Perfectionist)!

As Entertainers move toward immaturity, however, they become intensely competitive for all forms of success and prestige. Instead of developing themselves, they resort to projecting images that are meant to make a favorable impression on others. Pragmatic and calculating, they change their image to get what they want and attract admiration from others.

Immature Threes will also take advantage of people as they struggle to maintain their fake images. Extremely manipulative if they sense they might lose in a competition, they become jealous and aim to ruin other people's attempts at winning. Like the other types in this Triad, Threes also have a problem with hostility. Often they try to get even with anyone who is more successful than they. While Twos and Fours are indirectly hostile, Threes are more direct. They put down friends and betray colleagues. Those who sense their vindictiveness often give in to avoid getting on the bad side of a Three.

As immature Entertainers deteriorate, they build their self-concept around an inflated self-regard. They begin to love themselves in narcissistic ways. Of course, they are not really in love with themselves as much as they are with the image they project to others. Narcissists are incapable of empathizing with anyone's feelings or needs because they are interested only in themselves. This is why they're incapable of forming long, mutually satisfying relationships with others.

Mature Threes

At their best, mature Threes are self-accepting. They're no longer concerned about what others think of them. Here's their profile:

- Self-assured, confident and adaptable
- Charming and popular
- Ambitious to improve themselves
- Admirable, outstanding in some way but know their limitations
- Listen and speak well, persuasive
- Motivational, influential
- Direct, fast-paced and accomplished
- Authentic, enthusiastic and optimistic
- Dramatic in opinion and action

Average Threes

Average Threes are more interested in distinguishing themselves from others. They want to be seen as superior through competition. Their profile looks like this:

- Competitive, pragmatic, efficient and goal-oriented
- Like to compare themselves with others, with winning being critical
- Manipulative and calculating
- Image-conscious, concerned with "packaging" themselves
- More concerned with style than substance
- Inflated self-regard that leads to grandiose expectations and arrogance
- Use exaggeration and generalization to call attention to themselves

Immature Threes

Fear of failure motivates immature Entertainers who promote inflated images of themselves and then can't make good on their claims. Often they attempt to hold on to their inflated self-concepts by taking advantage of others. Their profile reads:

- Opportunistic, out for themselves, will exploit others
- Immoral, untrustworthy and not above "stabbing" colleagues and

friends in the back for their own gain
- Jealous, manipulative and devious
- Attempt to ruin those who win

When a mature Entertainer moves in the direction of a Six (the Disciple), they have worked through the fear of exposing their real selves and the possible consequences of their being rejected. They've also learned to commit to someone besides themselves — a traditionally frightening step for most Threes because it means that someone will find out that their projected image is false. When Entertainers move toward the Traditionalist level, they learn that their commitment to others does not diminish their self-image; it expands it by allowing them to become part of something greater than themselves. Through exposing their true selves, Threes discover they are still accepted. This acceptance of their true selves becomes a foundation from which they can grow.

The maturing direction for Entertainers is: 3→6→9.

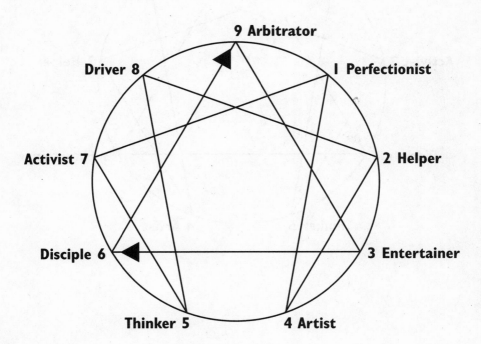

Immature Threes who deteriorate integrate the immature traits of the Nine (The Arbitrator). The major problem for immature Threes is that they are out of touch with their feelings, a situation made worse by any movement toward Nine. Threes on their way to Nine deteriorate into a "dream world" where everything becomes unreal. No longer vindictive toward others when they go to Nine, unhealthy Entertainers disassociate themselves from the only feelings they have (even hostile ones). The result is they feel nothing. They're "flat," without zest or energy. They are empty.

The deteriorating direction for Entertainers is: 3→9→6.

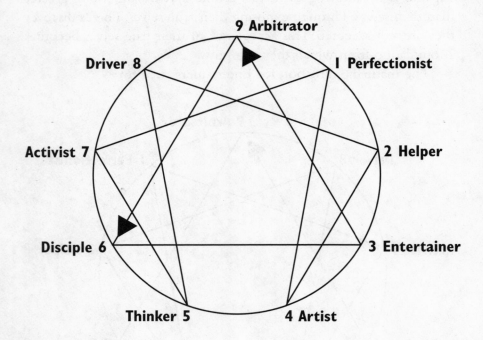

When Entertainers talk to themselves, here are some of the things they say:

My Basic Fear
"I fear being rejected."

My Basic Motivation
"I want to get better, rise above my competition, get attention and impress others. I will do anything to get on top and stay there."

Mature Sense of Who I Am
"I am a desirable, admirable person."

My Greatest Irritation
"I am a superior person who has worked hard to get where I am today and people don't recognize it — they are jealous."

The Spark That Ignites My Movement Toward Defensiveness
"I begin to compete with others over everything. I want to distinguish myself so when I fail, I can compare myself with others and still look down upon them. My sense of self-worth is very much tied to these comparisons even though I know I should measure my behavior against more objective principles and values."

My Greatest Sin
"I'm more interested in 'packaging' the product than the product itself. I project an image that will ensure my successes."

My Greatest Strength
"When I'm mature, I still love myself, but I invest the time and energy to develop myself without comparisons or competition. I accept my limitations."

The Entertainer at Work

Entertainers like to be treated with warmth, friendliness, and approval. They enjoy interacting with people on more than just a business level and are very good at selling themselves. You almost can't help being impressed. Entertainers know that once you've "bought" them, you'll buy their product, service or ideas. Goal-directed and impatient, they carry themselves in ways that reflect their optimism and fast pace.

Entertainers like to think out loud. Desks tend to confine them, so they typically move around the office talking to nearly everyone from the custodian to the boss, calling everybody by his or her first name. All the while they notice people's reactions to them and are especially excited when comments or stories involve them. Many people interpret the Entertainer's behavior as "goofing off" when in reality it is their vital mode of working. They are effective in brainstorming out loud with virtually everyone they encounter because this serves to reinforce the image that they are desirable people. They like feedback and the pats on the back that their conversations provide.

Because Entertainers are naturally talkative and people-oriented, they often seek positions where they can be included by others, achieve popularity and gain social recognition. They may be dreamers, but they're very good at getting others caught up in their ideas.

Because Entertainers want to be accepted and have learned to produce, they are good idea people. This often gets them in trouble. Other personality types may believe they have made a commitment while an Entertainer does not view the situation in the same way. "Okay, I've done my part—what about you?" is often met with, "What are you talking about? I never agreed to that! I was just thinking out loud."

Given the choice, Entertainers prefer to:
- Work with others
- Receive constant feedback and recognition
- Be on a first-name basis
- Hear compliments about themselves and their accomplishments
- Work in stimulating environments
- Work toward known, specific and quickly attainable ends

Strategies for Working With Entertainers

Entertainers tend to be communicative, warm, approachable and, at the same time, competitive. Expect them to share with you and others their ideas, feelings, etc. This behavior says they want you as a friend, but what they *really* want is for you to *follow* and *support* their dreams and share their vision. If they see you as a competitor or someone who is trying to take the credit away from them, they will try to get even with you. People are important to Entertainers because they use relationships to achieve and produce. Power and politics are often used by immature Threes to enhance their personal recognition and even recruit followers to their cause.

To work effectively with Entertainers:

1. Ask questions about their opinions and ideas. Let them share with you their vision of what they and others should do to achieve these ends, but avoid a results-oriented discussion where lots of facts and details are thrown about. Objectivity makes the Entertainer uncomfortable.

2. Look for ideas they find exciting and join with them in turning their ideas into successes you can both share.

3. Give them most of the credit for the development of any idea.

4. Don't compete or argue. Disagreements threaten Entertainers so much that winning the argument is more important than finding a solution. Rather than say "I disagree," opt for, "Here's another alternative," or "Here's another option you might consider."

5. When you reach agreement, be sure to work out the details with Entertainers: the who's, what's, when's, where's, whys and how's. If they are not interested in the details, summarize what's been discussed and suggest ideas for implementing what you have both agreed to.

6. Ask what you can do to help them put their ideas into action.

7. Present your ideas in a stimulating, entertaining, fast-moving, story-telling manner. Motivational stories about people and situations that support your ideas in a positive way go a long way with Entertainers, but be careful; You may end your discussion on an up-note without ever having reached your point. Entertainers are notorious for how easily they can change directions. Record your agreements on paper if possible. When work-

ing with Entertainers, make it your responsibility to take the initiative in maintaining the relationship on a friendly, enthusiastic note while at the same time pinning them down to details.

8. Support your ideas with the opinions of others. This means more to Entertainers about to make a decision than all the facts, details and substance you can provide. Show how other people and other organizations have benefited from the decisions you ask them to make. Entertainers respond well to incentives for making decisions and taking risks if they believe they will receive recognition for what they do.

If You're an Entertainer....

1. Develop a sense of cooperation in your relationships. Take the feelings of others into consideration and work with them to create collaborative results. You will be admired much more if you can make people feel they've played a major role in any decision.

2. Be honest about your accomplishments. Don't exaggerate or brag, and resist the temptation to inflate your own importance. People will respond more favorably to you if you genuinely share your glory.

3. Don't betray confidences or use secrets for your own advantage.

4. Guard against the "Entitlement Fallacy"—that just because you want something, you're entitled to it. Recognize that desire and obligations are different and that others have the right to say no to you. Remember the times when you had to say no to others. To help you cope with this tendency, tell yourself:
   • I am free to want, but they are free to say no.
   • I have my limits, but they do too.
   • I have the right to say no, and you do too.
   • My desire doesn't obligate you to meet it.

5. See yourself as unique. Many immature Threes are quick to clone themselves after "models" they perceive as successful. By avoiding the temptation to do what is acceptable, you can focus on developing your own strengths and correcting your own weaknesses.

6. Learn to support. Admiring others and congratulating them on their achievements will only bring recognition to you in return.

7. Use your energy, humor and enthusiasm for the benefit of others. They will reciprocate with appreciation and admiration.

8. Lower your expectations for adulation and acclaim. If people like what you do, they will tell you. If they don't, you may be thinking of yourself in a more favorable light than is realistic.

9. Be more cooperative and collaborative and less competitive. Your hostility grows out of your need to always compete and win. Because you can't win all the time, you set yourself up for becoming hostile and negative toward others. Be interdependent. You will win in more areas of your life if you think and work as a team member.

10. Don't measure your success against that of others. Focus instead on producing worthwhile work that benefits others. That's the key for becoming the best Entertainer you can be.

Chapter 6

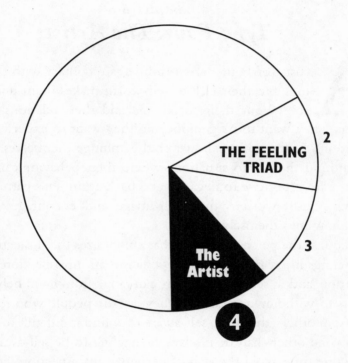

Man's greatest experience — the one that brings supreme
exultation — is spiritual, not physical. It is the catching of some
vision of the universe and translating it into a poem or work of art,
into a Sermon on the Mount, into a Gettysburg Address, into a
mathematical formula that unlocks the doors of atomic energy.
—William O. Douglas

Chapter 6
Type Four: The Artist

Artists (or Fours) are in immediate contact with their feelings, but their lack of self-worth makes them uncomfortable about their social role and their relationships with others. They want to be genuine and they want to experience deep emotions. In the process, however, they plunge themselves and others around them into situations where their behavior can quickly change from positive to negative and back again. This pattern disappoints Artists, worsens their self-image and encourages them to withdraw into themselves.

Four is the personality type that emphasizes the subjective world of feelings in creativity and individualism, in introspection and self-assertion, and in self-hatred. Fours can range from genuinely creative artists to withdrawn dreamers. They are the people who feel different from others; they're so self-aware they find it difficult to be aware of anyone other than themselves. Struggling to be self-aware and at the same time avoid the trap of perpetual introspection, Fours turn to art as a channel for expressing what they've learned about themselves. Without constricting their emotions, Mature Fours harness them to produce works of beauty while, in the process, discovering who they are. This is why all forms of creativity are valued by Fours.

The problem for Fours is that creativity is not a constant in anyone's life. This is why Artists moving toward maturity learn *not* to look into themselves but toward others; they need to work through the threat of moving beyond their own self-awareness.

Fours who move toward immaturity have the problem of trying too hard to understand themselves. As they move inward, their own emotional state becomes their own reality, and they communicate their feelings by creating art or adopting an aesthetic lifestyle. Early in their lives, Artists learned to deal with the ugly world around them by escaping into their imaginations, that haven where they could create plays, poems, music and other works of art through which they could channel their deep sensations.

The direction of the Four's personality heads inward as if pulled by a magnetic force. They know they are different from other people and they look inside constantly for an answer as to why they're different. The more withdrawn Fours become, the more difficulty they have coping with reality.

In mature Fours, we see people who are able to bridge their inner and outer sides. Because they can sense in themselves the depths to which people can descend as well as the heights to which people can ascend, no other personality type is so aware of the potentials and predicaments of human nature. This is why mature Fours create things that move people; able to get in touch with the hidden depths of human nature, they discover what is at the core in each of us.

Like Twos (Helpers) and Threes (Entertainers), Fours have a problem with hostility. Only, they direct their anger inward. Fearing that something is wrong with them, they use their self-directed anger as a defense against the fear. Having learned to doubt themselves and their worth at an early age, and angry with themselves for being defective, they punish themselves.

Mature Fours

Mature Fours are most in touch with the impulses from their unconscious and, at the same time, able to remain open to impressions made by their environments. Generally, they can be described as:

- Introspective
- "In touch" with their feelings and emotions
- Sensitive to themselves and others
- Compassionate
- Tactful
- Respectful of others

- Content with being alone
- Slower-paced than Helpers and Entertainers
- Emotionally honest and authentic
- Highly creative
- More intuitive than cerebral
- Able to discuss their fears
- Able to describe their internal states through outer media

Average Fours

Fearing that they will be misunderstood or that their feelings will be hurt if they express too much of themselves, average Fours seek other ways to express their feelings. Their profile reads:
- Self-absorbed to the point of shyness
- Interested in expressing their emotions indirectly
- Imaginative to the point of fantasizing
- Withdrawn in conflict
- Moody, easily hurt and not very practical
- Unable to easily express their feelings to others

Immature Fours

When their dreams and visions fail, immature Fours become angry at themselves because they realize that, in their quest to learn about themselves by going inward, they have lost precious time, missed many opportunities and have fallen behind others in almost every way — socially, personally and professionally. Immature Artists are:
- Depressed
- Angry at themselves
- Always fatigued
- Emotionally blocked
- Negative to the point of despairing
- Unable to discuss their ideas or feelings
- Not strongly connected with other people
- Uncomfortable with any kind of responsibility

Artists mature when they move 4→1→7→5→8→2 on the Enneagram.

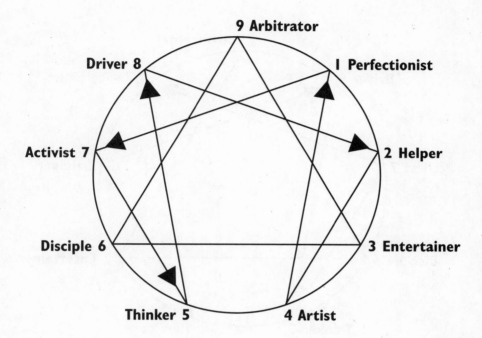

When Fours take on the mature traits of the One (The Perfectionist), they move from a world of subjectivity into a world of objectivity, from self-absorption to principled action. By confronting and working through their fear of being perceived by others as defective or inadequate and by building successes that are tangible and real without strong reference to their feelings, Artists learn to be controlled not by their feelings, but by their convictions.

Fours who have moved to One have accepted that there are values and expectations that we must all submit to. They willingly become self-disciplined, working consistently toward achieving their potential and cultivating their seed so they can contribute to the world.

Immature Fours deteriorate when they move in the direction of unhealthy Twos (Helpers). The Enneagram depicts their progress this way: 4→2→8→5→7→1.

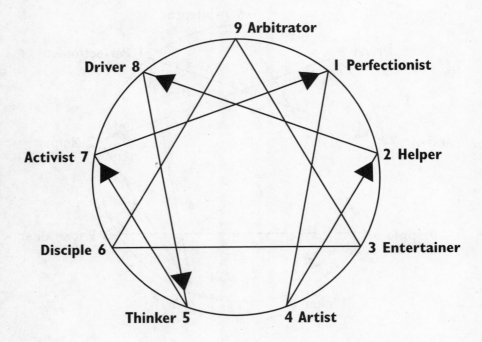

A deteriorating Four integrates the immature traits of the unhealthy Two (The Helper). Fours who deteriorate to this level have a strong desire to escape from themselves by becoming dependent on someone who will provide the love and understanding they believe they have missed. Although immature Fours typically withdraw, they still want and need people, so moving toward Two is an ironic acknowledgment of this need. The move to the Helper is a chance to overcome their sense of "self-alienation" by connecting with another person. The problem, however, is that immature Fours are incapable of entering into, much less sustaining, genuine relationships. Hating themselves, they aren't capable of loving anyone else.

Here are some of the things Fours often tell themselves:

My Basic Fear
"I fear being defective or inadequate in some way."

My Basic Motivation
"I want to understand who I am — my thoughts, my feelings, my unconscious — so I can become all that I'm capable of becoming."

Mature Sense of Who I Am
"I am an intuitive, sensitive person."

My Greatest Irritation
"I have always been misunderstood by others, and I've always looked inside to find understanding. Because people look at me as different, I've come to believe that I'm different, and it really upsets me when I feel I don't fit in."

The Spark That Ignites My Movement Toward Defensiveness:
"I begin to overuse my imagination as I search for self-understanding. I think that I will find myself and the meaning of my feelings by retreating into fantasies. I become too enamored with fantasies rather than deal with reality and thus I give myself permission to 'feel' and 'be' anything while wasting precious time in my life."

My Greatest Sin
"I'm jealous of others because they seem normal and able to fit in so easily."

My Greatest Strength
"When I'm mature, I achieve emotional balance in my life. I realize I'm able to solve the problems of my reality at home and work without feeling so vulnerable to my emotions. As a result of dealing with reality, I learn to problem-solve, to take action and turn negative situations into positive experiences."

At Work With the Artist

Artists want to create unique products and services. They prefer to work alone at their own pace and answer to their own standards and ideals.

Because they fear that they'll be perceived by others as inadequate if they don't create things of beauty, they are slow and methodical and keep their emotions to themselves or channel their feelings into their work. Artists are cautious thinkers and good at asking themselves questions. As might be expected, their answers come from introspection. In fact, their creative minds can become restrained by their need to monitor their feelings as they progress on any project. Because Artists fear failure in their quest for self-understanding—which is more important to them than the quest for actual results—they are very quick to become negative when faced with setbacks. Viewing setbacks as permanent, pervasive and the result of their own inadequacies, Artists easily lose hope because setbacks reinforce their concept that they are unworthy and deficient.

When positively motivated and mature, Artists consider the past and present as they prepare for tomorrow. Viewing each task in relation to the whole, they often alter some of their tasks so the outcome becomes somewhat different than before. In other words, they create.

Working With Artists

1. Artists tend to be warm, approachable people when mature, but distant to the point of being uncommunicative when immature. Because they are more cooperative than competitive, work to make them feel adequate, accepted and part of the team. Don't force them to involve themselves too quickly or they will reject you and your ideas. Be patient and give them the time they need to think. Support their feelings, intuitions and ideas, and build their confidence by reminding them of their past successes.

2. Because Artists tend to act slowly and don't make the best use of their time, use time to support their feelings, build relationships and strive for agreements. Be careful, however, not to move too

quickly. You can avoid this trap by supporting the Artists' feelings and ideas. Demonstrate in a casual way the worthiness of your Artists' ideas while supporting their feelings and intuition.

3. Because Artists are indecisive, they tend to base their choices on intuition. For this reason, the past plays a critical role in providing assurances that the decisions you ask them to make are correct. If you can point to the successful decisions made by Artists in the past while remaining sensitive to their mood, you can influence them to act more quickly on your recommendations.

Accepting Yourself as the Artist

1. Don't pay too much attention to your feelings. See them as a part of who you are. Who you are is much more than just your feelings.

2. Don't procrastinate on doing things until you are in the right mood. Commit yourself to working hard on something tangible that will contribute to the success of your organization and family. Successes in the real world count for more than those that occur only in your imagination.

3. Start small, do something worthy, and generate positive experiences that reinforce the idea that you are more than just your feelings. Take reasonable risks and learn the pleasure of success. See failure as an opportunity to try something different next time. Paying too much attention to your internal feelings in the face of failure will immobilize you from taking action, from solving problems and, most importantly, from maturing and growing.

4. Practice self-discipline. Sleep consistent hours, eat healthy foods and exercise regularly. Self-discipline is not an obstacle to your freedom. Because it comes from you, it creates energy where before there was only despair.

5. Avoid negative language in your thoughts; don't put yourself down.

6. Talk openly with the people whom you trust. Your goal is to learn that you're not that different or as much of an outsider as

you think. To contradict your inner negative beliefs, look outward toward others. Finding out who you are is as much an "outside search" as it is an "inside search."

7. Volunteer for projects and community activities; involve yourself in practical, noble pursuits.

8. Don't get caught up in complaining about the past: "I'm this way because..." Look instead to the future, use your self-understanding as a basis for growing and maturing. By changing your attitudes, beliefs and behavior, you can seize what the future holds for you.

9. Try not to take things personally. When your boss criticizes you, don't take it as being reflective of the whole truth about you. In fact, be less critical of yourself and more critical of remarks thrown your way.

10. You are a better friend to others than you are to yourself. Become a better friend to yourself.

PART III

DOERS

Chapter 7

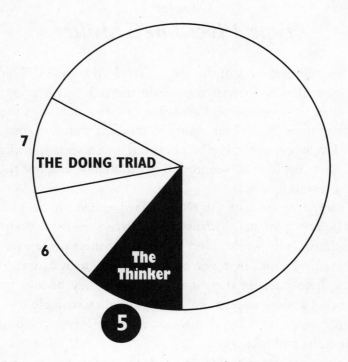

Knowest the true value of time. Snatch, seize and enjoy
every moment of it. No idleness, no laziness, no procrastination.
Never put off till tomorrow what you can do today.
—Lord Chesterfield

Chapter 7
Type Five: The Thinker

Fives are members of the Doing Triad. Also called "Thinkers," they like to analyze the world around them. They prefer thinking to doing and are often out of touch with the practical side of their lives. Their ability to translate impulses into action is underdeveloped and, therefore, Fives are often seen as withdrawn. In fact, they become so engrossed with their thoughts they can exclude everything else.

All three members of the Doing Triad — Fives (The Thinkers), Sixes (The Disciples) and Sevens (The Activists) — focus their attention on the outside world, then think about their perceptions. And that's their problem: Their perceptions are often inaccurate, which frustrates them because they won't act until they believe they are certain of what they want to do. As a result, they struggle to validate their perceptions, an effort that forces them to leave the comfort of their thoughts and take a risk.

Thinkers are characterized by a deep experience of emptiness. They would like to find fulfillment through intelligence and often find security in understanding and explanations. But they have trouble getting in touch with their feelings. The reason for this is that their feelings don't develop until a few days after the fact. In other words, it takes a while for experiences to enter their heads where, once there, they stay for a while. This is why Fives like "distance." Distance provides objectivity for healthy Fives; for unhealthy Fives it removes them from reality. Thinkers who become increasingly immature use distance to admit only the kinds of information that confirms their mental perception of the world. This often leads them to be narrow-minded, rigid and extremely conservative.

Like the other two members of the Doing Triad, immature Fives feel insecure when their environment is unpredictable and uncertain. To protect themselves, they become vigilant about their surroundings so they can anticipate problems before they occur. As they retreat into their intellectual world, Thinkers reduce complexity into simplicity. This gives them a sense of control, but the more they retreat, the more incapable they are of taking action and making things better.

When Fives are mature, they observe reality as it is and are able to comprehend complex phenomena at a glance. Immature Fives, on the other hand, reach premature conclusions about their environment by projecting their faulty interpretations on it. In their search for security, these Thinkers reduce complexity into a single, all-embracing idea so they can defend themselves by having everything figured out. Extremely immature Fives can become obsessed with completely disturbed notions about reality.

Fives also have a problem with anxiety, which is common to the types that make up this Triad. Afraid of allowing anyone or anything to influence their thoughts, they fear being controlled. Because their self-worth is based upon their ability to defend the validity of their ideas, they feel diminished if another person proves them wrong. To protect themselves, immature Thinkers resist testing their ideas in the real world. Not really knowing if their perceptions are correct, they often keep their thoughts to themselves.

Mature Fives

At their best, mature Fives see patterns where others see nothing but confusion. Able to synthesize existing knowledge and make connections between elements that no one previously knew were related, mature Thinkers do not cling to old theories or pet interpretations. This enables them to discover truths that would have remained mysteries. In other words, mature Thinkers are patient. They're willing to deal with uncertainty until all facts come in. Here's their profile:

● Mentally alert but more cerebral than intuitive
● Able to be objective and ask insightful questions

- Able to distinguish patterns and predict how current events will end
- Eager to learn, excited by knowing, willing to contribute
- Independent, innovative, visionary
- Prefers to work in a well-structured environment but can be personally unconventional, even idiosyncratic

Average Fives

The major difference between mature Fives and average Fives is that the latter fear they don't know enough about their subjects to act or to reveal their discoveries. Their profile looks like this:

- Specialized but more preoccupied with interpretation than actual data
- Constantly dissecting things intellectually but inclined to jump to conclusions
- Like "making a science" of things but interpret facts according to their theories
- Use details to build abstractions
- Poor interpersonal skills make them contentious when others disagree
- Need few "creature comforts"
- Under stress, retreat into thoughts
- Slower-paced, tentative, methodical

Immature Fives

Because immature Thinkers need to be correct about their interpretations of reality, they are often antagonistic toward those who disagree with them. This resentment increases when people question, ridicule or dismiss their ideas. Here's their profile:

- Reclusive, secretive and isolated from people and reality
- Fearful of others and antagonistic toward those who might disagree with them
- Self-contained, emotionally detached, often have difficulty connecting with people

- Not motivated to be socially acceptable, prone to arguments
- Distrusting of authority, suspicious of rules
- Keep their needs simple, avoid physical activity

When mature Thinkers take on the healthy traits of an Eight (the Driver), they have overcome their fear of their environments and begun to trust the world around them. As Thinkers learn to trust their environment, their confidence grows. They realize that, as little as they think they know, they still know a lot more than anyone else. They also discover that they don't need to know everything there is to know in order to act. As they turn more and more of their thoughts into action, Thinkers discover that objectivity and certitude are only illusions. Now able to put themselves on the line, Thinkers contribute beneficially to others. Their sequence on the Enneagram moves from 5→8→2→4→1→7.

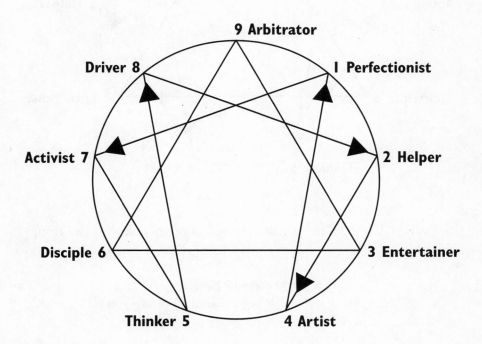

Deteriorating Fives integrate the immature traits of the Seven (The Disciple). They realize that too much thinking has inhibited them, so now they've decided to act. Unfortunately, their actions are impulsive. With so little thought behind them, those acts can range from the erratic to the hysterical. Quick to lunge at apparent solutions to their problems, immature Thinkers often do more harm than good. Their determination on the Enneagram looks like this: 5→7→1→4→2→8.

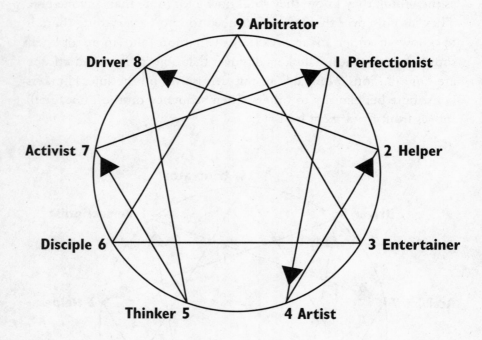

When Thinkers talk to themselves, here are some of the things they say:

My Basic Fear
"My view of reality will be invalidated by another person."

My Basic Motivation
"I want to understand the world around me — to observe everything, to be certain that my views are correct and to reject those views that don't agree with my unifying theory."

Mature Sense of Who I Am
"I am intelligent, perceptive and vigilant."

My Greatest Irritation
"I am so brilliant that no one is capable of coming close to the knowledge I possess; when someone questions my intelligence, I get really upset."

The Spark That Ignites My Movement Toward Defensiveness
"I analyze everything because, through analysis, I can control my environment, gain insight, make predictions about what is likely to happen, and protect myself if necessary. I become so focused on details, though, I begin to lose perspective."

My Greatest Sin
"I'm so hungry for knowledge that I've deluded myself into believing that more knowledge protects me from the world."

My Greatest Strength
"Understanding. I am able to comprehend many points of view at the same time. This enables me to be compassionate and tolerant of different viewpoints as opposed to cynical and detached."

At Work With the Thinker

Thinkers respond well to structured activity. They like orderly, systematic approaches to work through which they can understand everything. They like to ask questions, but they may be critical of those who are not as orderly and methodical. Their tendency is to move slowly and accurately because they need to be right. The more details, substance, specifics and facts they can amass, the more secure they feel. Unfortunately, they never feel secure enough to act, and they fail to make decisions or take action. In short, they are the world's busiest procrastinators.

For these reasons, Thinkers need to know that assignments need to be completed on time. Deadlines can't wait while Thinkers complete their careful study and analysis. Thinkers need to know that they must take more initiative and entertain greater risks in their relationships with others. Even though they don't like to impose their ideas on others, Thinkers need to be more decisive.

Thinkers prefer to be asked questions rather than seeking others out and giving advice. When they ask the questions, Thinkers focus on the details. A work setting that emphasizes an intellectual, consultative role is more to their liking than an authoritative or inspirational one. As Thinkers, beginning to integrate the mature traits of The Driver, they become quite able to lead others because they've learned to be comfortable with not being right all of the time. This confidence can translate into a great deal of power because employees learn that the leader is moving them in a direction that is most likely to generate success.

Strategies for Working With Thinkers

Because Thinkers are uncommunicative, independent and distant, they're cautious about making friends and are more concerned with getting things done. They prefer not rushing into a relationship until they understand how the relationship can be managed and controlled so they won't get hurt. With time, you can develop dedicated relationships with mature Thinkers, but you must earn their trust. They tend to be suspicious of power and avoid getting involved with those who have leverage. Only when they understand and can predict how that leverage will be used will they act. If Thinkers see power used in a systematic, orchestrated way to achieve stated goals, they identify strongly with its use and may even use this power in their own efforts to achieve results.

To relate effectively with Thinkers:

1. Demonstrate that you are willing to help them by your actions rather than your words. For example, you may wish to prepare a written presentation of the thoughts you would like your Thinkers *to consider* before making various decisions.

2. Focus on specifics, facts, details and substance; don't oversell, and do what you say you will do. List the advantages and disadvantages of plans you make along with *suggested* ways of overcoming the disadvantages.

3. Don't rush Thinkers into making a decision before they have had ample time to review the decision for themselves.

4. Agree on a schedule for the implementation of an idea, and make sure you write down the who's, what's, when's, where's, why's and how's of your plan.

5. If you disagree with Thinkers, argue on the basis of facts and be careful not to use the word "disagree" with them; don't push too hard that you are correct and they are wrong.

6. Acknowledge the Thinker's competence by making statements such as, "I respect your viewpoint because I consider you an expert..." but be prepared to have your statement be disregarded if your opinion, in the Thinker's mind, is inconsequential.

7. Give Thinkers time to reflect. For example, you might say to a Thinker, "Cindy, from our discussion, I think I know what you're looking for. It's well thought out and may be the direction we ultimately go in. Give me some time to think it through, and while I'm considering this, let me ask you if you can take some time to consider some of my ideas. Maybe you can work them into something." This accomplishes two things; first, you give Thinkers more time to consider alternative views without putting them on the defensive by forcing them to accept your ideas, and, second, a break in the interaction gives you the chance to regroup and remind yourself that the objective is to get something done.

8. Encourage Thinkers to consider alternative viewpoints without threatening them. One way to do this is by presenting *alternatives* to the Thinker as *detours*. In other words, you may wish to say, "I realize that this may not be what we end up with, but could we take a few minutes just to see if there might be anything useful in it?" Another way to encourage Thinkers to extend their concepts or theories over time and space is to ask, "How will that

concept look in practice?" or "Can you tell me how that will look in a year?" These kinds of questions move your discussion from the conceptual level to the concrete level.

9. Because Thinkers are highly disciplined but slow to act, they may come across as uncooperative. Typically if you are in a hurry, it's their slow pace and your frustration with their slow pace that tells you that they are uncooperative people. Thinkers can be cooperative as long as you're prepared. Knowing the facts and details of a situation shows the Thinker that you've been thinking about your interaction. This will work to your advantage, because Thinkers often check to see if people know what they're talking about.

10. Try not to be too flashy. If you are not making the progress you believe you should be making with a Thinker, find out what he or she would like to see in terms of additional detail. Then provide the necessary detail in a systematic manner. Your ability to get accurate facts and provide them to the Thinker in a logical, predictable way will strengthen your relationship.

11. Thinkers are risk averse. To successfully influence a Thinker, provide evidence that what you say is based on substance, not someone's opinion. Thinkers want to be sure that any decision made today will be just as valid in the future, so any evidence you can provide them that the future will not deteriorate will go a long way toward getting the Thinker to agree with you and support your position.

12. Don't rush Thinkers into making decisions. Avoid testimonials from other people, gimmicks, quick manipulations and personal incentives as levers in getting them to decide. Be patient, slow and methodical like them. Recognize that, while it may take a little longer to decide, the decision will probably turn out to be right and, in the process, you've earned the respect and trust of your Thinker.

**Suggestions for Becoming
More Accepting as the Thinker**

1. You want to understand your environment, but your under-standing becomes distorted when you try to impose preconcep-tions on it rather than observing it. Therefore, analyze less and observe more.

2. You tend to be intense and high-strung and find it difficult to relax and unwind. Make an effort to calm down. Try to exercise more and think less.

3. You see many alternatives when you need to make a decision, but you have a difficult time deciding which one is best. Even mature Fives have to work at this. Using the advice of someone whose judgment you trust will be difficult but critical in enabling you to take a risk and, even more importantly, teaching you that it's okay to trust people.

4 Don't jump to conclusions. Be open to new information as it comes in and use it to modify your original theories.

5. You tend not to trust people or open up to them. This creates a self-fulfilling prophecy. Recognize that conflict is not unusual and that the mature behavior is to work conflicts out rather than withdrawing from them. Having one or two close friends whom you trust enough to have conflicts with will help you adjust to conflict with others.

6. Try to be more cooperative. Learn to yield without feeling that you have been beaten intellectually or that you have been put in a vulnerable position.

7. Your brilliance may intimidate others and make them feel uncomfortable. Because you're so wrapped up in your ideas and what interests you, you forget the basic social courtesies. Try to remember them by thinking how others see you or how you feel when you are slighted.

8. You can benefit by sharing your insights with others, especially when your views are critical to understanding a problem. Offer realistic, logical suggestions that have a probability of making things better, even if your solutions aren't perfect.

9. Be less critical and demanding of yourself and others. Accept the fact that reality and life are not perfect; accept the fact that you're not perfect.

10. You have an enormous ability to understand. By combining your insight into people with compassion, your own gentle feelings will emerge and soften your hard edges. You will become more trusting, relaxed and happier if you identify with people rather than observing and analyzing their every move. In other words, don't just use your head, use your heart as well. It will make you more mature.

Chapter 8

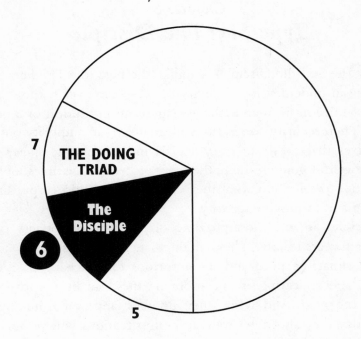

We all surrender some part of our personality to the organization....
The important thing is not so much the organization's pressures
as the need to be aware of them. What's devastating is the number
of people who find organization ideas superior to their own.
They surrender and they enjoy it.

—John Kenneth Galbraith

Chapter 8
Type Six: The Disciple

The Six (the Disciple) — unlike the Five (the Thinker) with an underdeveloped ability to act — can't act without permission from an authority figure, an institution or a belief system. Their security comes from allegiance to an authority outside themselves that they can obey. By having something bigger and more powerful guiding them, they feel protected. Disciples look to authorities to tell them what they can and cannot do, to put limits on them and to provide security.

Disciples are the most puzzling of the nine personality types because they are reactive. They can fluctuate from one state to another at an amazing speed and are notorious for reversing positions. Lovable and endearing at one moment, they can be negative and cranky the next. And while they do seek approval from higher authorities, they also don't want to be in situations where they feel inferior. They may be obedient and then openly disobedient, deviating from what an authority has told them to do. As a result, Disciples are the most contradictory of the nine personality types. Those who best know them say they are easy to like but hard to get to know.

The key to unlocking Disciples' personality lies in one word: *ambivalent*. They can feel simultaneously strong and weak, dependent and independent, passive and aggressive. As with Dr. Jekyll and Mr. Hyde, it is difficult to predict the state Disciples will be in from one moment to the next. To make matters worse, Sixes are ambivalent toward themselves: one moment they like themselves and the next moment they don't; one moment they're confident, the next, they're insecure.

As Sixes oscillate from one emotional state to another, there seems to be little stability. Not only do they look outside themselves for direction, but also the actions they take are often indecisive and circuitous. All three personality types of the Doing Triad have a problem with anxiety, but Sixes have the biggest problem of all, because they are aware of their anxiety. Sometimes they resist it, and sometimes they succumb to it.

Along with anxiety, average-to-immature Disciples feel an insecurity that develops out of their ambivalence. They don't know how they feel about people; while they want to like other people, they are suspicious of those who might not like them in return. To make matters worse, average-to-immature Sixes don't have a good handle on how others view them. They'll consequently seek approval as a way to test others' attitudes.

Think of Sixes as a mixture of extroverted and introverted feelings (ambiverts). This is why they react to whatever they have done (especially if anxiety is produced) by doing the opposite as a means to compensate. They then react to the new state and then to the next and the next, ad infinitum. Here's a typical scenario: A Disciple seeks to get approval from the boss by doing a special report; then, fearing that he will be taken advantage of, the Disciple becomes suspicious of the boss—the very person whose approval is being sought. Now, becoming anxious about these suspicions, the Disciple seeks reassurance from the boss that things are all right. With reassurance given, the Disciple begins to wonder if he has not been too ingratiating and overcompensates by getting defensive with the boss—acting as if the boss' approval was of no consequence to him. Get the picture? If you have a hard time understanding someone who is a mass of contradictions, you are probably dealing with a Six.

Early in their lives, Disciples learned that they couldn't trust themselves. As a result, they're very short on confidence. This causes them to look outside for people and institutions they can trust. Sixes need to be told every day to trust themselves. Under most circumstances they will protect and support what they believe in, won't demand any special recognition and have no grand plans. Silent and industrious, Sixes do what they are told.

Mature Sixes

At their best, mature Disciples learn to affirm themselves. The self-affirmation comes from realizing their own value without reference to anyone else. This is an important shift for Sixes to make because they no longer see all the world's good residing in others.

Here's the profile:

- Identify strongly with others and want to form lasting bonds of trust and friendship
- Practical, down-to-earth and hard-working
- Disciplined, organized and able to follow through on details
- Loyal and committed to those they believe in
- Generally positive, self-affirming
- Dependable, responsible and trustworthy
- Independent, yet function well in groups

Average Sixes

Once Sixes become loyal to a person or group, they may, however, fear taking responsibility for themselves. Before they act, average Sixes want to feel secure by adhering to the rules of the group and to have the approval of others—especially an authority figure. Average Sixes are neither independent nor do they want to be. They want boundaries set for them by an authority and don't care whether the authority is a person or a set of rules. Their profile reads:

- Afraid to make decisions
- Obedient to authorities
- Afraid to assume responsibility for their behavior
- Ambivalent—shifting from one viewpoint to the next
- Need to know what is expected of them
- Stress importance of social obligations
- Stand by friends even when they are wrong
- Seek advice from others when uncertain about what to do
- Need reassurance from others in difficult situations

Immature Sixes

As a means of handling their ambivalence and its resulting anxiety—
not to mention their fear of seeming inferior, immature Disciples
will often act aggressively toward those from whom they seek
approval. If they act too aggressively, Sixes may fear that they have
jeopardized their relationship with the authority and will suffer serious consequences. Although they may not have done anything serious, they fear they have. As a result, their fear immobilizes them from
taking productive and independent stances; instead they seek reas-
surances that no matter what they have done in the past, their relationship with their authority figure is still intact. Their profile
includes:

- Need pressure to force action because of difficulty in making decisions
- Are skeptical about people until they are able to be trusted
- Fear being taken advantage of
- Procrastinating until pressure makes them worry
- Reacting strongly to too much pressure
- Complaining when others don't "pull their weight"
- Stubborn and defensive
- Hate those who break the rules and get away with it
- Dependent and possibly clinging
- Feel inferior, put themselves down

When Sixes move toward maturity, their sequence on the
Enneagram reads: 6→9→3.

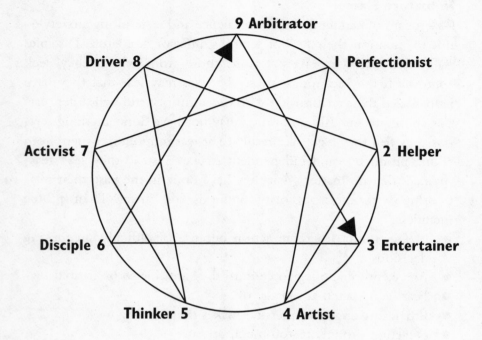

Mature Sixes take on the healthy traits of the Nine (The Arbitrator) when they have resolved their ambivalence and anxiety about themselves and others. At Nine, The Six is more open, receptive and sympathetic toward people. As a result, his or her emotional spectrum grows wider. Disciples at this stage have overcome their tendency to be dependent without losing their status as people on whom others can rely. Now able to support and reassure others rather than merely seek their reassurance and support, these Disciples make trustworthy friends who give as well as receive. People seek them out because they are so healthy, mature and accessible. The playfulness and sense of humor we see in mature Disciples has not been left behind when a Six goes to Nine. Rather, these qualities mold with an optimism and kindheartedness. Sixes at Nine are secure, trusting of themselves and able to trust others.

Movement Toward Defensive Direction

Immature Sixes who deteriorate take on the immature traits of the Three (The Entertainer). No longer do these immature Disciples disparage themselves and masochistically turn their aggression inward; instead they go after others to see them suffer. They feel their aggression has been building for some time and often take it out on others to compensate for having been passive themselves. Whereas once — as Disciples—Sixes wanted only protection and security from others, now they're willing to strike out at those whom they believe have hurt them.

Immature Disciples mark their deteriorating on the Enneagram with the sequence: 6→3→9.

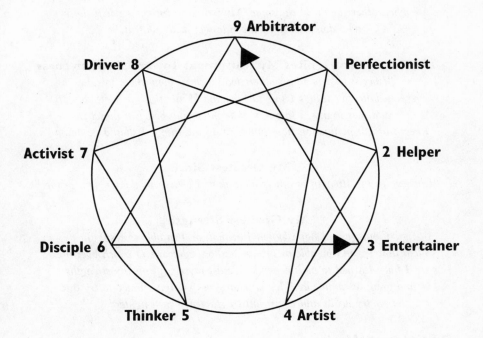

Here are some of the messages Disciples send to themselves:

My Basic Fear
"People will abandon me and I'll be alone."

My Basic Motivation
*"I want to be liked, to get approval from others, to test their attitudes;
but more than anything else, I want security in my life."*

Mature Sense of Who I Am
*"I am a likable, dependable, reliable person who contributes
to the betterment of the people and institutions I believe in."*

My Greatest Irritation
*"I follow the rules and expectations of others and am irritated
when others don't do the same. My irritation increases when those
who don't abide by the rules get away with it."*

The Spark That Ignites My Movement Toward Defensiveness
*"I begin to depend on others too much. I allow them to take
responsibility for things I should be doing. While this gives me comfort
and reassurance, I know it undermines my belief in myself;
I begin to ask permission from others to do the things I should be doing."*

My Greatest Sin
"I believe in the strength of others more than I believe in the strength of me."

My Greatest Strength
*"Courage and hope. When I'm mature, I'm able to resist the
fear that I won't be able to survive without someone to watch over me.
I have learned to be independent, trust myself, affirm my strengths
and grow in confidence. This is what gives me the courage to try and
try again and again until I succeed. I'm a fighter."*

Disciples at Work
- Want organization, respect and acceptance
- Are naturally reserved and supporting
- Fear loss of security

- Follow established rules and traditions
- Prefer sticking to limited activities within a specified period of time and following through until these activities are completed
- Think logically and realistically
- Prefer tangible, identifiable tasks
- Will comply under pressure

Disciples are quiet and reserved; they'd rather listen and ask questions than talk. Typically, they keep their opinions to themselves. When asked to take a stand, they become tentative, quiet and indecisive. At times they will be seen as wishy-washy, tight-lipped and unassertive. Less confrontational, less demanding, and less competitive than most, they're team players who allow others to take the initiative. Often supportive of others, Disciples have an above-average range of vocal inflection, make continual eye contact and speak in terms of feelings. Other supporting behaviors include animated facial expressions, hand and body movements and a tendency to tell stories and anecdotes.

The Disciples' greatest need is security; their greatest fears are disorganization and changes in the status quo. Where others may look before they leap, Disciples look before they step. They think, plan ahead and tend to follow established patterns where they work. They also like to see projects through to completion. Disciples like being asked for advice and, assuming they've accomplished the same task before, will most likely show the questioner an organized, step-by-step procedure that works for them. If they've never done a certain task before, they will show the questioner the accepted or normal way it is done.

Disciples accentuate the positive. When they work on a task, they go about it in a predetermined manner and with a rather easygoing approach. They know what to do and they do it, usually without being sidetracked. Consistent and pleasant in their work style, they contribute positively to any team effort.

Disciples naturally want to provide services and favors for people. For example, they are willing to assemble parts and materials for a project, saving others time and energy. They like to see others getting along and supporting each other. In their efforts to keep relationships stable, Disciples can be especially tolerant and accommodating. More often than not, they give people the benefit of the doubt.

Because Disciples often look on the bright side and seek the best in people, they are capable of covering up someone's unacceptable actions or overlooking the possibility that the person may be taking advantage of them.

Strategies for Working With Disciples

1. Disciples are communicative, warm and approachable—open people who want to cooperate with you in a team or group effort that will contribute to the overall effectiveness of the organization. Disciples bring stability and perseverance to their workplace because they want peace and harmony in their lives. Although comfortable in most work environments, they may become too comfortable with using the same old methods again and again. Sometimes their procedures include unnecessary steps that may have been needed when they first learned the procedure but now can be discarded.

   When they learn new tasks, Disciples favor one-on-one, hands-on instruction with real live human beings. Starting at the beginning and ending at the end, they learn each step, one at a time, until they are comfortable with what they're doing. When learning, Disciples tend to observe others for longer than average amounts of time. Only when they feel confident that they will be able to perform a task successfully will they take the first step to begin.

2. Tell Disciples how dependable they are, how highly others regard them, how well they get along with people and how important their efforts have been to the organization. Effusiveness can cause Disciples to be suspicious, so stick to praising what they've done in practical terms rather than speaking in terms of more abstract, personal attributes.

3. Be ready to do more of the talking than listening with Disciples, who don't always feel comfortable when the limelight is on them. State clearly your expectations and present your instructions in an organized, easy-to-follow manner. Make sure you both agree on what was said. When giving feedback, assure Disciples that you want to correct a specific behavior, not them. They take things personally, so remove the "something is wrong with you" barrier as soon as possible. Don't blame or judge them as people; focus instead on the behavior. If the problem involves a procedure, help them learn how to improve it. Point out what they're doing right while emphasizing what needs to be changed for the betterment of themselves and the group.

4. When acknowledging the Disciple, focus on how much you appreciate their willingness to work hard to make themselves and others better. Approach matters in a systematic, low-key manner. Also, indicate how you have noticed they make the most valuable contribution when they take the initiative to share their own ideas and insight with others.

5. Allow plenty of time for Disciples to explore their thoughts and feelings so you can understand the emotional side of their situation. Disciples are not usually forthcoming, so draw them out through questions and listening. Keep in mind they don't like sudden change—good or bad—and that stability is their most important issue. Reduce their fears by showing how specific changes will benefit them and the organization.

6. Disciples are risk-averse, indecisive and slow to make decisions. Focus on one subject at a time, one step at a time. Make sure they understand at all times what their role is in the decision-making process. Encourage them to share their opinions and suggestions as to how a decision is likely to add even more stability to the current condition. When suggesting a different possibility to Disciples, point out how you are trying to identify ways that you can be helpful and continue to make things pleasant for them.

Suggestions for Becoming More Accepting as a Disciple

1. Try to remember that anxiety is something everyone has. Learn to use your anxiety, to explore it and come to terms with it.

2. Try not to be defensive and testy. You get edgy when you're upset and angry, and you have a tendency to blame others for things you have brought on yourself. When you're in a bad mood, resist the temptation to think negatively and whine. Realize that you are often your own worst enemy.

3. You tend to overreact under stress. Learn to identify what makes you overreact. Also realize that few of the things you fear have come true.

4. Become more trusting. You have a gift for getting people to like you, but you are uncertain of yourself and may be afraid of making a commitment to them. Let people know how you feel about them!

5. Accept responsibility more gracefully and maturely. People respect those who take responsibility for their actions, especially if they have made a mistake. If you try avoiding responsibility, you may alienate others.

6. You want to feel secure, but this will never happen until you feel secure with yourself. You often get into patterns where you believe that setbacks are permanent, pervasive and personal; reverse this cycle by affirming yourself and believing in yourself, which will happen only if you take risks and build successes in handling tough people and situations.

7. Respect authority but do not worship it. Ingratiating yourself to someone in authority will get you nowhere in the long run with anyone worth associating with. If someone is looking for a team player who will do anything they are told, it should not be you. That kind of authority is most likely to see you as expendable as soon as they're done using you.

8. What irritates others and undermines your relationships is that you often give mixed signals. Be fair. Let them know what's on your mind.

Chapter 9

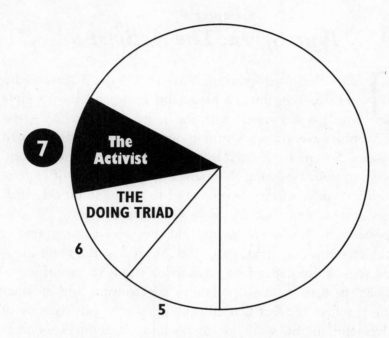

The trouble with the rat race is

even if you win, you're still a rat.

—Lily Tomlin

Chapter 9
Type Seven: The Activist

U nlike the other types in this Triad—the Thinker who tends to substitute thinking for doing and the Disciple who has lost touch with his or her ability to act—the Activist overdoes everything. Spinning out of control in their search for happiness, Sevens are excited by their surroundings and respond strongly to stimuli. Throwing themselves into the world of experience with incredible vitality, Sevens react to things so quickly that, regardless of what they do, they rarely slow down.

Experience is the Sevens' guide, and they are at home among tastes, colors, sounds and textures of the material world. Their identities and self-esteem depend on obtaining a steady stream of sensations. Their personality traits, defensive mechanisms and all their motivations reflect the fact that all things desirable exist outside of themselves and in the world of things and experiences. Neither introspective nor especially good with people, Activists are experience-oriented. Extroverted, practical and materialistic, they feel the world exists for their pleasure.

When Sevens are mature, their experiences are a great source of joy, and they learn to do many things well because their focus is on producing something in the environment. As they become immature, however, Sevens turn away from being productive to possessing and consuming more experiences. Increasingly hyperactive, they never really get a chance to enjoy their immediate experiences. If their deterioration continues, Sevens use their hyperactivity to escape the stress associated with working through problems. At this stage, they are often said to be "out of control."

The self-image of an Activist is, "I'm a happy and cheerful person," but the Activist's deeper motive is fear of pain. Afraid of the dark and painful side of reality, they are well known for changing the subject when a serious subject arises. In short, they refuse to feel pain.

Activists are practical and often accomplished. Their positive, even joyous orientation to the world often creates happiness for themselves and others. But if their appetites get the best of them, they will consume more than they need and certainly more than they can appreciate. They begin to enjoy their experiences less while anxious about obtaining more of everything.

As their pleasure in experience decreases, immature Sevens feel anxious and insecure — the common problems of the Doing Triad — and become increasingly more active. As they become hyperactive, Sevens grow even more anxious and insecure. This cycle intensifies with time. Because they are extroverted, however, Activists do not tolerate anxiety. Nor do they care to examine what causes their anxiety. This would draw them inward, which, being extroverted, is exactly where they don't want to go. As a result, they tend to repress their anxiety and seek more activities. Unfortunately, the more activities they participate in to repress their feelings of anxiety, the less satisfying these experiences are. Ultimately, Activists can find little satisfaction in anything they do. When they realize they may never be satisfied, they panic and become enraged because life hasn't provided the happiness they sought.

Average Sevens want instant gratification. They place no limits on themselves and deny themselves nothing. If they see something they want, they must have it. If something occurs to them that they must do, they have to do it now! They have strong wants. Sevens are notorious for putting people in a position of having to place limits on them instead of doing it themselves. Frustrated by these outer-imposed limits, Sevens become enraged and move quickly into conflict.

Mature Sevens, in contrast, concern themselves with the satisfaction of their genuine needs rather than the gratification of every desire. They are producers, not consumers. They are fairly happy people who have learned to get in touch with their feelings and with themselves. When they don't learn self-control, though, their appetites run amok and they become greedy, selfish and insensitive.

Mature Sevens

At their best, mature Sevens realize they don't have to expect happiness every time they have an experience. They discover that whatever life holds is enough to satisfy them. Reality, with its daily experiences, makes them not only happy but impels them to go beyond accepting reality and affirming it as it is. The profile of a mature Activist contains these characteristics:

- Highly responsive, excitable and enthusiastic
- Extroverted, oriented to things and sensations outside themselves
- Spontaneous and exhilarated by activity
- Happy, vivacious, sociable and physically active
- Multi-talented, Renaissance people with an eye on the future
- Storyteller and entertainer
- Appreciative of what life has to offer
- Practical, productive and willing to take risks

Average Sevens

Because their experiences are so gratifying to them, average Sevens fear that if they focus on one or two things, they will miss out on others. So they want more of those things that made them happy. In a sense, their eyes get bigger than their stomachs. They try everything at least once so they can see and do it all and avoid the anxiety that results when they're deprived of experiences. The major difference between a mature Seven and an average Seven is that the average Seven is less productive, more materialistic and less genuinely accomplished. Their profile reads:

- Avid consumers who use money to participate in experiences
- Materialistic, seeking to be comfortable at home and at work ·
- Sensation-seekers who can't deny themselves anything they want
- Hyperactive, superficial and flamboyant
- Loud and boisterous; talking, joking and performing constantly

to keep their spirits high
- Greedy, self-centered, able to consider different alternatives before making a decision
- Able to juggle many things at once

Immature Sevens

Because they don't reflect on their experiences, immature Sevens are at a loss to figure out why they're unhappy and dissatisfied, especially when they own so many of the good things in life. Frustrated, they "strike out" at those people who they have identified as getting in the way of what they want. They continue to stay in motion, although now their motion is escapist. They'll do anything if it promises to make them happy or serves to relieve their anxiety. Their profile is:

- Easily and quickly frustrated
- Offensive and abusive toward others in order to get what they want
- Impulsive, outspoken, having little self-control
- Erratic, volatile mood swings; capable of temper tantrums
- Skeptical and disparaging of those who can't keep up with them
- Look to binges to compensate for anxiety that has built up inside of them
- Push the limits because they are rarely satisfied with what they have

When mature Activists take on the mature traits of the Five (the Thinker), they go beneath the surface of their experiences. Because they no longer fear being deprived and have learned to appreciate what life has to offer, Mature Sevens at Five now have the anchors they need to find stability and security in their lives. Sevens at Five want to know more about the experiences that make them happy; they become more respectful of the integrity of everything and understand that the world and its experiences are not there exclusively for their personal consumption. Sevens at Five concentrate on quality experiences and gaining validity in the satisfaction they receive.

Activists who move in healthy directions follow the 7→5→8→2→4→1 sequence on the Enneagram.

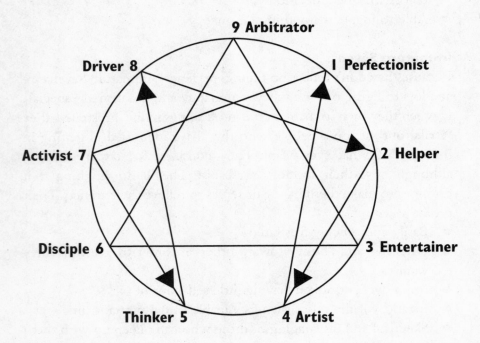

An immature Seven who deteriorates takes on the immature traits of the One (the Perfectionist). As we've said, immature Sevens are panic-stricken and out of control. When they move to One, they throw all their energy into some direction or plan that they hope will provide them a sense of control over their world. Self-control, however, is what they need most. So the move to One is their last-ditch effort at getting control. Intensifying their interest in a thing or person into an obsession, they become manic. Going to One also provides the rationale to punish anyone (typically the object of their obsession) who does not give them what they want.

Their sequence on the Enneagram reads: 7→1→4→2→8→5.

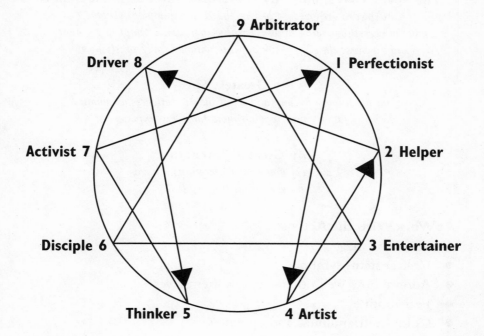

When Activists listen to themselves, here's what they hear:

My Basic Fear
"I fear being deprived of life's experiences."

My Basic Motivation
*"I want more than anything else to be happy and satisfied.
I want to have fun, be amused and do anything
(without limits) that blocks whatever stress I feel.*

Mature Sense of Who I Am
"I am a happy, enthusiastic, vivacious person."

My Greatest Irritation
"I am happy but I'd be happier if I got everything I wanted."

The Spark That Ignites My Movement Toward Defensiveness
"I start to get greedy. I believe that I'll be happier if I have
more of everything, but I'm also learning that, as I attempt to get more,
I only increase the size of my appetite without really satisfying it."

My Greatest Sin
"I am too hungry for any and all of life's experiences as opposed
to being hungry for fewer but more satisfying experiences."

My Greatest Strength
"I am very grateful for everything I have.
I believe life itself is a gift."

At Work With the Activist

Activists at work:

- Collect status symbols
- Admire how well others express themselves
- Fear routine
- Cultivate friendliness and openness
- Are optimistic and positive
- Need freedom
- Become aggressive toward those in their way

Activists at work are generally direct people. Motivated to pursue a variety of activities and projects in their search for happiness, they prefer activities that provide them the freedom and power to generate materialistic rewards: high salary, being on a first-name basis with the boss and other tangible items that will encourage people to comment on their prestige.

In addition, Activists want freedom. Confinement and restrictions make them very uncomfortable and aggressive toward those they identify as responsible for "holding" them back. Because they tend to be free spirits, Activists prefer setting their own limits for tasks, schedules, etc.

Activists are optimistic. They like others who are able to express themselves well and, at times, can be overly helpful with those who are less verbal. Activists are the people who complete your sentences for you or explain what you mean to others.

When things go wrong or people disappoint them, Activists continue to be optimistic. Unless, of course, they're immature. Then they'll rationalize excuses for the situation or for others.

Mature Activists are confident. They can handle criticism, don't require others' good wishes to maintain their enthusiasm, tend to act young at heart and are able to view each new person and situation as interesting. Their ability to see life as continually fresh keeps them open. When they're mature, they are less cynical and skeptical than any of the other personality types. Because they know they can be aggressive at times, they accept the same behavior in others.

Strategies for Working With Activists

1. Activists are communicative, spontaneous, fun-loving people who are motivated by a quick-paced environment, and you want to be entertaining and fast-moving with them. At work, Activists like to know everyone's name and something about them. They benefit from feedback by coworkers and contribute energy and enthusiasm to most projects. Activists are "open books" and easily read; just look at their faces.

2. As true extroverts, Activists look outside themselves to renew their energies. They enjoy tapes, videos and books to recharge their batteries and prefer the word *opportunity* or *challenge* to the word *problem*. A "problem" is too mired in negativism to fit with the optimistic nature of the Activist.

3. Here are some general strategies in working with Activists:
    *   Support their opinions, ideas and dreams.
    *   Don't move so fast with them that you lose focus of what's been agreed to.
    *   Try not to argue; if you do have a disagreement, offer other ideas and options.
    *   Summarize in writing what has been agreed to.
    *   Use testimonials to positively affect decisions.

- Plan to be stimulating in your conversations and show interest in them.
- Meet them boldly, and don't be shy. Introduce yourself first. Bring up new topics openly.
- When you propose solutions, use stories and illustrations that relate to them and their goals.
- When complimenting them, single them out as individuals.
- When counseling them, allow them plenty of opportunity to talk about things that are bothering them. Listen for facts and feelings. Probe with direct questions. Many times Activists just need to ventilate.
- Be clear and specific about what you expect in terms of results. Establish check points to prevent Activists from going off on tangents. The more involved they are in agreeing on expectations and execution strategies, the more they'll adhere to any.

4. Control their time and emotions by developing a more objective mindset. Activists benefit from spending more time checking, verifying, specifying and organizing. Otherwise, they fall prey to the "Ready, Fire, Aim!" tendency.

   Often Activists have so many things going on, they forget to finish tasks on time, or they procrastinate until the last minute because of their multiple priorities. Writing things down and prioritizing can help them remember when to do what with whom.

5. As inductive thinkers, Activists naturally see the big picture first, then the supporting details. After seeing the broad overview, they prefer not to get tied down to specifics. Decisive risk-takers, they want adventure, not analysis. They want to try out different alternatives before being forced to make a decision. Provide them with options and alternatives, paint a picture of the future state of affairs with each alternative, give them time to experience for themselves the options, and let them decide which one is best. Then provide testimonials to confirm their choice. Don't provide testimonials too soon. Unless they're asked for, the Activists

will think you're forcing them too quickly into your preferred option.

When you allow the Activist to experience each alternative, limit their time, and write down what's next in the process. Make sure you both agree in terms of the specifics.

Suggestions for Becoming More Accepting as the Activist
1. Try not to be impulsive.
2. Learn to listen to other people. They are often interesting and you can learn a lot. Know that silence and solitude are okay; you don't have to be the life of every party.
3. You don't have to have everything now! Most good opportunities will come back again and you will be in a better position to discern which opportunities are best for you. Distance yourself from impulsive decisions and learn to be vigilant about the consequences of those impulses that you chose not to act on.
4. Select quality over quantity in your experiences.
5. Use your strengths as a planner to ensure that what you really want now will be good for you in the long run. The worst thing is to want something now and—because you failed to consider the future—that something becomes a source of unhappiness.
6. Do not make happiness a goal. Consider it a by-product of committing yourself to something worthwhile.
7. Because you are so naturally enthusiastic, be careful about losing control.
8. When focusing on tasks, be objective in your analysis of situations and attend to both facts and feelings.
9. Find ways to give rather than get. Material possessions will never satisfy you, and you will never have all that you want. Even if you could, how could a "thing" provide fulfillment? Persons are not "things." The only "thing" that can really satisfy a person is a relationship with another person. Learn to give and learn to experience the joy other people receive when they relate with you.

PART IV

RELATERS

Chapter 10

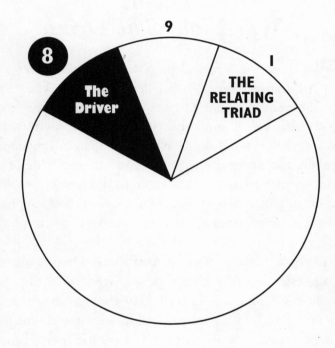

The world little knows or cares how many storms
the ship met at sea. It only wants to know
did the captain bring the ship safely to port?
—LaSalle Leffall, M.D.

Chapter 10
Type Eight: The Driver

The Relating Triad depicts ways that Drivers (Type 8), Arbitrators (Type 9) and Perfectionists (Type 1) relate to their environment. Drivers want to dominate it, Arbitrators want to coexist with it and Perfectionists want to perfect it.

Drivers are direct and aggressive. Larger than life, they make their presence felt, and make you pay attention to them. When they rumble into a room, you know they've arrived. They know it, too, and they like it. In fact, much of their seemingly endless supply of energy comes from experiencing their strength and noticing how others respond.

Of all the types described in this book, Drivers are the most openly aggressive. As take-charge people who enjoy imposing their will on the environment—including, of course, other people—they are difficult to deal with because getting what they want is so critical to them. When they are mature, Drivers use their immense self-confidence and will to make things better. If they are immature, however, whatever power Drivers have deteriorates into a desire to prevail over others simply for the sake of overcoming them.

Drivers develop confidence because they succeed. Unfortunately, their ability to assert themselves can be destructive when their strong wills get out of hand. They don't realize that by asserting themselves at every opportunity, they dominate others, treat them inhumanly and, in the process, become inhuman themselves.

Drivers assert themselves until they achieve their goals. As long as their egos are kept in check, their behavior benefits others. As natural leaders who may become great leaders if their goals extend far enough beyond themselves to benefit others, Drivers can often inspire others to direct their energies in worthwhile pursuits.

Unfortunately, many Drivers are little more than egomaniacs. Pitting themselves against others in struggles for power and dominance, Drivers feel they are the only ones who can do things the way they should be done, and everyone else, consequently, should follow their example. And their orders. It is not surprising then, that immature Drivers are often dangerous when they become ruthlessly aggressive in the pursuit of their own goals.

Mature Eights

At their best, mature Eights restrain their self-assertion. They master their passions, repress their egos and, in proving by example the depth of their genuine strengths, they inspire others. Their profile reads:

- Assertive, self-confident and oriented to act
- Decisive and authoritative, able to command respect
- Resourceful self-starters, with energy that is contagious
- Provide, sponsor and promote worthwhile causes
- Heroic

Average Eights

The difference between a mature Eight and an average Eight is that the interests of a mature Eight coincide with the interests of others, whereas those of an average Eight do not. The aggressive side of assertion emerges in the desire of average Eights to act in their own self-interest. Check out their profile:

- Described as "rugged individualists" and "wheeler-dealers" who use their power to promote their own self-interest
- Audacious, adventurous and willing to take the risks necessary to dominate their environments
- Forceful and aggressive, and proud—to the point of being egomaniacal
- Confrontational and belligerent, and not afraid to use threats and fear of reprisal to get compliance from others
- Enjoy keeping others off balance and insecure

Immature Eights

The difference between average Eights and immature Eights is that average Eights need people and are willing to give them something in return for their obedience and cooperation. On the other hand, immature Eights are completely ruthless, despotic and tyrannical. "Might makes right" is their philosophy. To round out the profile, they are:

- Ruthless, violent and immoral, with no guilt and with fear of little or nothing
- Dictatorial, reckless and seemingly invincible, and subscribe totally to the "law of the jungle"

When mature Eights move in the direction of a Two (the Helper), they use their power and strength for others rather than against them. They become caring, generous, and personally concerned. By identifying with others, mature Drivers learn that all people are worthy of the same rights and privileges as they seek for themselves.

The maturing direction for Drivers is: 8→2→4→1→7→5.

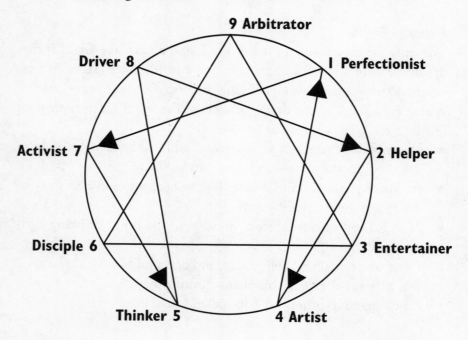

When immature Eights deteriorate, they take on immature characteristics of the Five (the Thinker). Thought becomes a tactical retrenchment from belligerent action. Now they can plan better and act less recklessly. By becoming more secretive, they will be able to strike without warning; by becoming more withdrawn, they will be able to hide from their enemies until they are ready to destroy them. The Enneagram depicts their progress this way: 8→5→7→1→4→2.

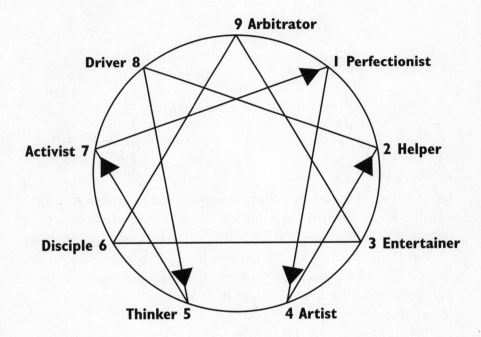

Here are some of the things Eights tell themselves:

My Basic Fear
"I fear submitting to others."

My Basic Motivation
"I want to be self-reliant by asserting myself and proving to others that I should be listened to. I want respect from others, to dominate the environment, even to be feared by others if necessary."

Mature Sense of Who I Am
"I am a strong, assertive person."

My Greatest Irritation
"I fight for my own survival and I know there are others out there who would take advantage of me if I let them."

The Spark That Ignites My Movement Toward Defensiveness
"I begin to believe that I'm entirely self-sufficient."

My Greatest Sin
"I begin to lust for power. I begin to feel that I need to possess and control others."

My Greatest Strength
Generosity. When I'm mature, I have a large heart. I can take the needs of others into equal consideration."

At Work With the Driver

Drivers at work are independent, strong-willed, restless and goal-oriented. Because of their drive for specific and concrete results, they often put in long hours. Their high-results orientation can manifest itself in an overextended work pattern, however. When this happens, Drivers pay a high price for their success: Their personal and social lives fall apart from neglect while their work-related achievements accumulate.

When Drivers perceive that the output from others is less than exemplary, their reaction is swift and direct: "Do something!" Drivers often demonstrate administrative and leadership qualities that reflect their ability to initiate, accomplish and then juggle several tasks simultaneously. As the pressure mounts to keep increasing numbers of tasks going all at the same time, however, Drivers start to emphasize quantity of the tasks rather than the quality of the results.

Although most people see the sense in putting one task on hold to relieve the pressure, Drivers can't admit to themselves that they might not be able to do everything all of the time. That would destroy their self-image. Before that happens, Drivers will get bored or complain about there not being enough hours in the day and then drop everything to head in new directions for their activities. When these new tasks become overwhelming, the pattern repeats. Drivers call this "reordering your priorities."

Drivers initiate action and their actions are clear, but their personal reasons are often a mystery to anyone who doesn't know they are Drivers. As a result, others can develop some uneasiness about the meaning of their independent, competitive behavior. Drivers, for example, aren't warm, friendly or personable. They're too busy getting things done. Many people feel intuitively that Drivers don't want them as friends. And they're right! Unless, of course, the Driver they're dealing with is mature.

Working With Drivers

1. Don't ever try to change the mind of a Driver. At least not directly. Support their objectives and give them alternatives they can choose from.

2. Ask specific questions. Drivers want to get things done. So focus on the actions and results that must take place for Drivers to reach their objectives.

3. Don't assume anything about the goals and objectives of Drivers and don't second-guess what they want. Look instead for specific ways you can help them reach their stated objectives. Keep everything businesslike and don't try to build a personal relationship with a Driver unless he or she indicates this is their objective.

4. If you disagree with the specific objectives of Drivers, take issue with the facts, not with them! And make sure your facts — as opposed to your philosophy — are not only accurate but support the Drivers' objectives. In other words, avoid personalities and focus on results.

5. Indicate all you can do and would like to do to achieve the Driver's objective. Then ask the Driver which of these actions he or she would like you to perform.

6. If you can't agree with conclusions of a Driver, explain directly why you can't agree and indicate what actions you see as realistic alternatives.

Suggestions for Becoming More Accepting as a Driver

1. Act with more self-restraint. You are at your best when you take charge and help others through crises. Few will take advantage of you and you will do more to secure the loyalty and devotion of others by showing mercy rather than your considerable "raw power."

2. You are not the only person in the world. Others have the same needs and rights as you. Ignore or violate their rights and they will fear you, lose respect for you and hate you.

3. Learn to yield to others. When little is at stake, you can afford to let others have their way.

4. You want to be self-reliant and independent, but you need the cooperation of others to accomplish your goals. Recognize that your self-sufficiency is an illusion.

5. You place too much value on money as a source of power and as a sign of achievement. Learn to serve a higher purpose. Consider ways to improve your relationships with the people who are important to you.

6. One of your greatest potentials is your ability to create opportunities for others. Think of the harm you can do to others; then think of the good. By which do you wish to be remembered? Make this goal a passion.

7. Seek the viewpoints of others in goal-setting and problem-solving situations. And don't be judgmental!

Chapter 11

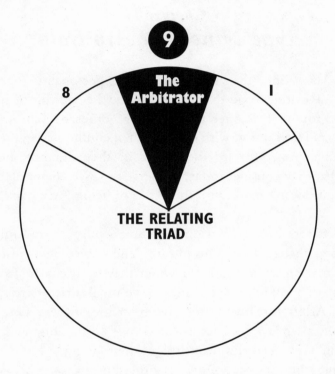

Negotiation is the exchange of ideas for the purpose
of influencing behavior.... Wishes are converted into reality
through the cold water of bargaining.

—Chester Krass

Chapter 11
Type Nine: The Arbitrator

The Nine (the Arbitrator) is the personality type in the Relating Triad that prefers to coexist with his or her environment. Rather than confront other people, Arbitrators identify and find union with others. When conflicts arise, they either direct their anger toward themselves or they distance themselves from what they consider to be a negative situation. Fighting for what they want doesn't mesh with their idea of being loving and satisfied people.

Arbitrators have a hard time finding a purpose and mission in life. Apt to change mountains into molehills, they fail to place much importance on anything. Even when they're forced to face a real problem, they often miss it. While active in all sorts of activities and hobbies, Arbitrators invest little energy in any of them. For this reason, many people see Nines as lazy. Prone to nicotine and caffeine addiction, they need stimulants to get them going.

While Ones (Perfectionists) take the shortest route between two points, Nines go off on tangents and then decide their original destination isn't important. Often they can't decide where to go in the first place. This is why they can be so unnerving to people. Sometimes you want to shake them and ask, "Who are you, and what do you actually want?" Well, they don't know what they want—one thing is as good as another.

Although they can drive us crazy with their lack of commitment, Arbitrators are likeable souls because they rarely get carried away by their own impulses. If you're an Entertainer, for example, Arbitrators will participate in your entertainment activities even if these activities are out of "sync" with who they are. In short,

Arbitrators are game for whatever is going on.

Nines are uncomplicated; their intentions are almost always clear. Once they make a decision , they'll stick to it at all costs. Think of the donkey as the symbolic animal of the Nine. Once it digs in its hind legs, it is difficult to move. What you see with a Nine is what you get.

Mature Nines

At their best, mature Nines allow themselves to be independent. Having overcome their fear of separation from others, they become self-possessed and autonomous. They are fulfilled and content because they are in union with someone from whom they can never be separated: themselves. Their profile looks like this:

- Self-accepting and accepting of others
- Easygoing, assuring, empathetic and supportive
- Good listeners, offering a calm, healing influence
- Excellent at bringing diverse groups together
- Good mediators

Average Nines

Average Nines act pretty much the same as mature Arbitrators; the difference is in their attitude. Because they subordinate the roles they play to a wide range of social conventions, average Arbitrators value themselves as others seem to value them. As a result, they're afraid to assert themselves. Their profile reads:

- Accommodating, submissive and often too willing to play conventional roles
- Passive to the point of conservative; conservative to the point of fearing change
- Passive, compliant, willing to walk away from problems
- Unable to focus and indifferent, with a tendency to procrastinate
- Inattentive, unreflective and stoic; often show poor judgment, tend to idolize others and look for magical solutions to ordinary problems

Immature Nines

Immature Nines often refuse to face problems and conflicts, thereby protecting themselves from anxiety and guilt and maintaining their illusions. Obstinate, neglectful and impervious to change, immature Arbitrators often do not act and often do not want to act. Their profile presents them as:

- Repressed to the point of helplessness
- Obstinate to the point of denial
- Neglectful to the point of irresponsibility

Arbitrators mature when they move 9→3→6 on the Enneagram:

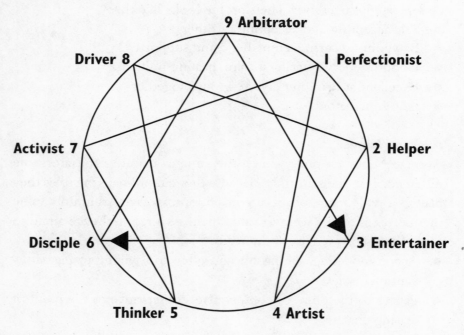

When mature Arbitrators move in the direction of Threes (Entertainers), they become self-assured and interested in developing themselves to their fullest potential. They move from self-possession to making something more of themselves, from a just-being-born presence in the world to an active, inner-directed force. Because they are already mature, they no longer try to live up to the expectations of others. Instead, they assert themselves more, welcome change and are more flexible in their dealings with the real world.

Immature Arbitrators deteriorate when they move in the direction of unhealthy Sixes (Disciples). The Enneagram depicts their progress this way: 9→6→3.

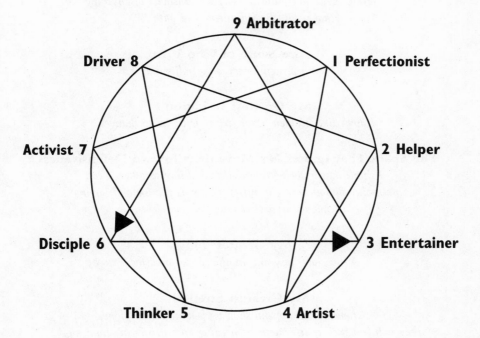

When immature Arbitrators integrate the immature traits of Disciples, anxiety has finally broken through their repression. All the Feelings they've been warding off come crashing down upon them with a vengeance. The once easygoing Arbitrator is now overreactive, hysterical, anxiety-ridden, fearful, agitated, apprehensive, tearful and panicked. More than ever, immature Nines who have deteriorated to Sixes need others to take care of them and save them from whatever situations they've gotten themselves into.

Here are some of the things Nines tell themselves:

My Basic Fear
"I fear being separated from others."

My Basic Motivation
"I want harmony and peace, to mediate conflicts and bring people together. I also want to preserve things as they are, to minimize conflict, and to deny the existence of anything that would be difficult to deal with."

Mature Sense of Who I Am
"I am a peaceful, easygoing individual."

My Greatest Irritation
"I don't like it when people try to force me to change."

The Spark That Ignites My Movement Toward Defensiveness
"I think that by being conciliatory and nice to others I can maintain relationships, but others see me as passive and having a tendency to neglect important problems."

My Greatest Sin
"I'm slow, lazy and indifferent to problems."

My Greatest Strength
"Patience. I am hopeful that, by leaving things alone, they will run their courses without needing any interference from me."

The Arbitrator at Work

In business and their personal lives, Arbitrators take it one day at a time. Consciously avoiding any uncertainty, they have a high regard for tradition. Because nothing in the workplace motivates them as much as stability, Arbitrators, along with their Helpers cousins, are most compatible with the idea of maintaining conflict-free relationships with others.

Arbitrators don't want to make waves and especially don't want to be perceived as "know-it-alls"; consequently, they avoid sending negative messages to others. Even if they fear they're being exploited to an unfair degree, they don't tell anyone! They'll just keep performing their jobs and making the best of an unfortunate situation.

If they are asked to make a presentation, mature Arbitrators will thoroughly prepare and dutifully organize their material. With their heavy reliance on proven methods, they will learn each step of any procedure so they can duplicate it later. Their overconcern with the process of instruction and convention, however, can limit their actions and creativity. Because Arbitrators favor step-by-step proceedings, they're natural choices for tutoring others, maintaining existing performance levels and organizing systems.

Note: Maintaining harmonic relationships and following established procedures both get high marks from Arbitrators. When problems occur, mature Arbitrators try to work with others in the use of tried-and-true solutions; immature Arbitrators withdraw and allow the problems to resolve themselves.

Inherently modest and accommodating, Arbitrators think their actions speak for themselves. They may want to divulge their part in activities with successful outcomes, but they won't volunteer the information.

Arbitrators bring to the workplace highly developed planning skills, consistent pace and a desire to fit in. Like Entertainers and Helpers, they prefer working with people on a casual, first-name basis. Unfortunately, they can become overly dependent on traditional methods and fall into rigid routines.

Because Arbitrators want union with others, they don't like to apply pressure or tell people what to do. Great listeners and empathizers, they often cannot bring themselves to ask a best friend to return an item by a specific time.

Here are some tips for dealing more effectively with Arbitrators:
1. Encourage them to become more straightforward with others in sharing their own expectations, ideas or reactions. Their preference for the indirect, more subtle approach encourages others to consciously or unconsciously take advantage of them. One way to motivate Arbitrators to open up is by asking them "open-ended" questions, questions that can't be answered with a single word or gesture.

2. Help Arbitrators monitor their tendency to tolerate others to the point of becoming their victim.

3. Set time limits when holding discussions with Arbitrators. Time limits pressure them to say what they'd rather keep to themselves.

4. Make Arbitrators personally responsible for completing the tasks assigned to them. Their natural optimism may delude them into underestimating the time it takes them to complete a project. Work with them to commit and attend to specifics: dates, times, objectives, constraints and deadlines.

Strategies for Helping the Arbitrator in You

1. Recognize your need to go along with others and do what they want to keep the peace. The ease with which you submit to others, however, will not build the kinds of relationships that will make you happy.

2. Be more assertive. Pay attention to the needs of others, but be willing to participate more in the decisions made to satisfy those needs.

3. Accept the fact that you have pent-up aggressions and anxieties. Get them out in the open and discover that the consequences for doing so are not nearly as severe as you think.

4. One of the great tragedies for Nines is that they may come to the end of their lives and realize that they never truly lived. It is as if their lives happened to someone else. Learn to accept the magnitude of your life and what it's like to be alive.

5. Share your feelings with your spouse and friends. Have confidence that you will not damage relationships with others by being human.

6. One of your greatest strengths is your receptivity to people. Others feel safe and comfortable around you. But they will love you more if you are willing to give something of yourself.

Chapter 12

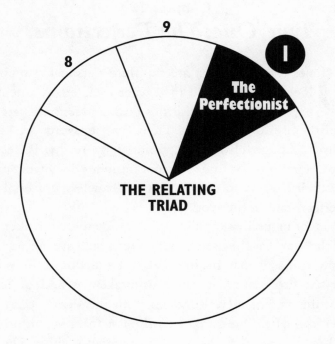

A perfectionist is someone who takes great pains in everything he or she does and gives them to everyone else.
—Anonymous

Chapter 12
Type One: The Perfectionist

Ones (Perfectionists) are the third personality type in the Relating Triad, and they want their environment to be perfect. To accomplish this goal, Perfectionists are highly critical of themselves and others. Their favorite words are "should" and "must." Though always disappointed by reality, Perfectionists never give up hope. As their disappointments inevitably pile up, however, their frustration thickens into a shapeless, universal rage at the imperfect state of the world.

This anger naturally supplies Perfectionists with lots of energy to improve the world as they see it, but it's an aggressive, negative energy. As powerful as it may be, the rage of Perfectionists doesn't look like rage. At first glance, it can be mistaken as zeal or idealism. Ironically, this rage is as well hidden from the Perfectionist as it is from everyone else. One's are often the last to know and the most surprised to discover that their major downfall is anger. The reason for this is that Ones are convinced they're pursuing high ideals and noble goals. What they need to learn is that their definitions of idealism and nobility are just that—their own definitions.

Subconsciously, Perfectionists live a life of anger that they neither recognize nor admit. This anger causes them to make snap judgments that often lead to a continual state of resentment. And the process quickly turns into a pattern: anger→judgment→resentment. This is why Perfectionists need to learn to intervene in the process when they feel anger; they need to acknowledge it as anger and then confront it with language that is less threatening and stringent. Instead of saying, "I must," or "I should," Perfectionists need to tell themselves, "It would be nice to," which is less likely to induce a perception of failure (and anger) if what is wanted is not achieved.

Perfectionists must learn to discover the imperfections in their narrow view of reality. This is no easy task when everything in the world is constantly framed by commandments and prohibitions. They need to learn that everything cannot be either good or bad, meritorious or sinful. When Perfectionists learn to be more tolerant of themselves and others, they begin to experience less anger and move toward increasingly greater levels of tranquility and cheer.

Mature Ones

Mature Ones allow their humanity to surface; they discover that their impulses are not as chaotic or as threatening as they had feared. Their subjective side comes into alignment with objective reality, and they become exceptionally realistic and tolerant — even of themselves. Because they are realistic people, mature Ones are also well balanced. Still attracted to their ideals, though, mature Ones no longer see them as stifling commands but rather as virtues that can be personally fulfilling. Recognizing that Perfectionism is an unattainable state, Perfectionists are profiled as:

- Conscientious, highly ethical, with a deep sense of right and wrong
- Reasonable, self-disciplined, placing high value on truth and justice
- Principled almost to a fault; can be counted on to be impartial, fair and objective
- Wise and discerning, often demonstrating great ability to evaluate and order well their priorities
- Tolerant, at their best, of own and others' shortcomings

Average Ones

Guided by their consciences, Perfectionists frequently subject themselves to guilt and anxiety. If for some reason they fear they are not living up to their moral principles as perfectly as they should, they begin to strive for excellence in everything. They become idealists, crusaders and missionaries. Exhorting themselves and others toward perpetual improvement, they plague them with their impossible images of what the world and everything in it should be. Their profile reads:

- High-minded and idealistic, but afraid of making mistakes

- Orderly, logical and detailed but rigid, impersonal and emotionally constricted
- Puritanical and opinionated, with a tendency to badger others to improve their imperfect states

Immature Ones

Immature Ones are always right and let no one ever make the mistake of trying to prove them wrong. Their ideals have become sterile absolutes that refuse to bend regardless of the situation. The difference between immature Ones and other Perfectionists is that, on occasion, the other Perfectionists include themselves in their criticism and feel guilty about their failed attempts at perfection. The profile of these self-righteous Perfectionists stack up like this:

- Dogmatic, inflexible; feel confident when judging others
- Often use rationalizations to maintain their "logical" position
- Cruel and sadistic at their worst; enjoy proving others wrong

Perfectionists mature when they move 1→7→5→8→2→4 on the Enneagram:

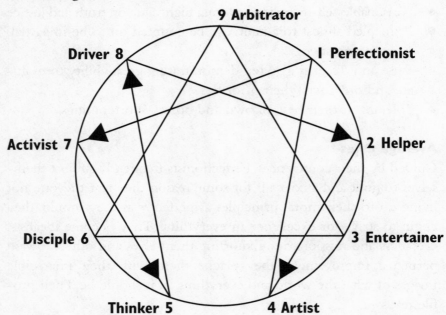

When mature Perfectionists evidence the mature traits of Sevens (Activists), they have learned to relax and appreciate the joy of life. They've learned to trust themselves and reality, to become life-affirming rather than controlling and rigid. They discover that life is not always grim and serious; happiness is possible. No longer obsessed with making everything perfect, they progress from obligation to enthusiasm, from constraint to freedom of action. Once relaxed and able to express their feelings spontaneously, mature Ones at Seven are responsive, playful and happy.

When immature Perfectionists deteriorate, however, they move in the direction of unhealthy Fours (Artists). The Enneagram depicts their negative progress this way: 1→4→2→8→5→7.

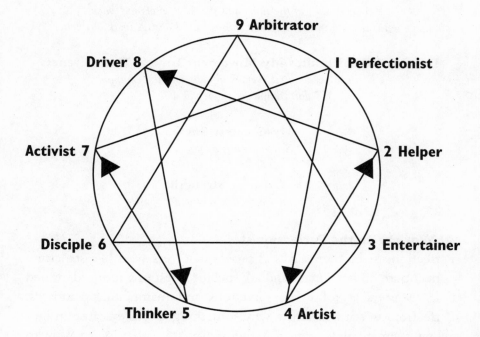

By pursuing an abstract ideal without any compassion for humanity, those Perfectionists do something so contradictory they realize they have failed. Profound guilt quickly follows and reduces the One to a helpless, depressed state.

What Perfectionists say to themselves:

My Basic Fear
"I'm afraid of being proved wrong."

My Basic Motivation
*"To be right, to improve the world, to control everything
so there won't be any mistakes, and to condemn others
who don't live up to my ideals."*

Mature Sense of Who I Am
"I am a reasonable, objective, fair person."

My Greatest Irritation
*"I'm right most of the time, and it really upsets me when
others don't listen to me. If they did, things would always work out better."*

The Spark That Ignites My Movement Toward Defensiveness
*"I begin to believe that everything falls on me to improve.
If I don't improve it, nobody will."*

My Greatest Sin
"Self-righteous anger."

My Greatest Strength
"I am wise when mature."

At Work With the Perfectionist

Perfectionists see themselves as problem-solvers who like structure, concentrate on key details and ask specific questions about identified tasks. Masters at following directions and maintaining standards, Perfectionists want to know why something works, because insight allows them to determine for themselves the most logical way to achieve expected results — for themselves as well as others.

Practical, process-oriented and willing to take only the lowest of risks, Perfectionists over-plan when change becomes inevitable. They prefer to work in those existing circumstances that promote quality products and services. Whenever possible, they prepare ahead of time for their projects and follow their work plans diligently. And just to make sure there are no slipups, they incorporate extra time in their schedules to accommodate the expected last-minute glitches.

Perfectionists rely on their extraordinary rational powers and heightened sense of discipline to avoid mistakes, so they tend to check, double-check and check again. Often they become so involved with data collection and analysis they limit their ability to offer options. They'll also hold onto important partial information until they've exhausted all their resources. This frustrates people who want to know what's going on now — like Drivers, Activists and Entertainers. In their minds, Perfectionists disrupt the work flow. Perfectionists can benefit from focusing more on what's critical and less on everything else. By sorting out and controlling the important details, they could still get things done well. And on time! Perfectionists need to accept the fact that perfectionism is an impossible quest and learn to settle for mere excellence instead.

Perfectionists tend to be introverted individuals whose natural orientation is toward objects and away from people. People, unlike objects, are unpredictable, complicated and difficult to understand. For this reason, Perfectionists prefer to work with colleagues who are calm, diligent and thorough: other Perfectionists, Thinkers, even Relaters. These other behavior types help Perfectionists modify their quest into more time-efficient procedures. Drivers, for example, help by maintaining deadlines; Entertainers help the Perfectionist lighten up, to realize there is more to the workplace than work.

When encouraged — they won't do it on their own — Perfectionists will share their rich supplies of information with small groups of coworkers. Sharing their wealth of experience and knowledge enhances the Perfectionists' status with colleagues and serves as a bridge toward teamwork and mutual understanding. Sharing also lessens the Perfectionists' reservations about coworkers and establishes a standard by which they can measure themselves against the very people they'd prefer to avoid.

Perfectionists avoid conflict. They prefer peace and tranquility and try to avoid outward expressions of anger. Immature Perfectionists sometimes will numb themselves so effectively against conflict they no longer know what they really feel — not only anger and hatred but caring and love as well.

By learning to accept the different ways people express themselves, Perfectionists also learn to accept their own feelings. By raising their tolerance levels for aggression, they correspondingly increase their ability to participate in mutual exchanges.

Here are some tips for dealing more effectively with Perfectionists:

1. Perfectionists don't like making decisions until they know they're 100 percent correct and they're not going to hurt anyone. Here is the kind of question you can use to encourage them to be more direct: "Even a good project has some things about it that are not quite as good as the best project. Could we talk about those?" Keep in mind that what Perfectionists share with you is probably what's keeping them from making a decision that needs to be made.

2. Persuade Perfectionists to limit the number of alternatives they're willing to consider. Try to limit their choices to two. More than two can immobilize any Perfectionist.

3. Link your plan to values of quality and service. Indicate why your idea is effective and be prepared to support your proposal with facts and details that will encourage the Perfectionist to act.

4. Support any correct decision — Perfectionists don't make many mistakes — by providing evidence that the choice they made was the right one.

5. Maintain as much control of any project as possible — especially the time frame. Perfectionists will delay everything they can until the last minute — there's always a chance it won't be perfect. If there is no "last possible moment," there will be no decision and no completed project.

Strategies for Helping the Perfectionist in You

1. Learn to relax. Recognize that the world around you will not

crumble if you are not perfect. Try to be content with being merely excellent.

2. You have a lot to teach others and probably are a good teacher, but don't expect others to change immediately. What is obvious to you may not be obvious to them, especially if they are not used to being as self-disciplined and objective as you are.

3. Keep in mind that you are not without your own faults and shortcomings; stop criticizing everyone else.

4. You get angry when others don't behave in ways you expect them to. Recognize that your definition of "the right way" is often just *different* from someone else's definition. Accept the fact that you love to play "judge and jury" and that, when you do it, you often create more problems than you solve.

5. Listen to others. They can be right too!

6. Stop driving people crazy with your impossibly high standards and inability to meet deadlines. Learn to accept the views of others, to settle for less in your work and to make yourself receptive to experiencing the joys of collaboration. You do not have to be perfect to be good.

PART V

SUMMARY

Chapter 13

If I had to live my life over again, I'd dare to make more mistakes next time.

I'd relax. I would limber up. I would be sillier than I have been this trip.

I would take fewer things seriously.

I would take more chances. I would take more trips.

I would climb more mountains, swim more rivers.

I would eat more ice cream and less beans.

I would perhaps have more actual troubles,

but I'd have fewer imaginary ones.

You see, I'm one of those people who lives seriously and sanely,

hour after hour, day after day. Oh, I've had my moments.

And if I had it to do over again, I'd have more of them.

In fact, I'd try to have nothing else, just moments, one after

another, instead of living so many years ahead of each day.

I've been one of those persons who never goes anywhere without

a thermometer, a hot water bottle, a raincoat, and a parachute.

If I had it to do again, I would travel lighter than I have.

If I had to live my life over, I would start barefoot earlier in the Spring

and stay that way later in the Fall.

I would go to more dances. I would ride more merry-go-rounds.

I would pick more daisies.

—Nadine Stair, who was in her eighties when she wrote it.

Chapter 13
A Final Word on Making the Enneagram Work for You

Do you remember when you learned how to drive a stick-shift automobile? John does, and his memories are very sad indeed! In 1973, he was 16 years old and living outside Boston in Waltham. He learned how to drive on a Volkswagen Beetle, black in color, no heat and with only half a floor board! On that fateful day his Dad said to him, "Do you want to learn how to drive?"

"Dad, that's not even a car; it's a lawn mower!"

"Get in the car. We're going to the high school parking lot."

"Why?"

"Because it's big!"

"That's negative....."; you get the drift, we've all been there.

They got to the high school parking lot and John's dad, still behind the wheel, began to show his son the procedure — depressing the clutch, shifting, and so on. "So," he said, "What do you think?"

Being a teenager and not short on brashness, John replied, "Are you kidding me? It's my turn!"

John has since told his Dad many times how impressed he was with the initial patience he displayed. Emphasis on the word *initial*, because when John took the wheel on the driver's side, he didn't know how or why, but he literally froze. Initial patience quickly turned to incredible impatience. We don't mean to stereotype, but Mr. Mattone is Italian from Brooklyn. Get the picture? After about 10 second of the freeze, John felt a smack on his shoulder. He was afraid to look. Another 10 seconds — then another smack. Now John turned to look at his father. "Do something," his father said. "Do something. Now!"

"I don't know what to do!"

"Turn the key and step down on the ❀ ¶X★#@ clutch!" John looked down to find the clutch and couldn't believe his eyes. "Dad, there's three pedals, and I've only got two feet! There's no way I or anyone else with two feet can drive a car with three pedals. There's no way; I can't do it!"

But something else was also taking place. Because John was known to never give up and because he was able to handle his Dad's particular kind of feedback — he became callous — he started to generate little successes, references that caused him to question the validity of his belief that he couldn't drive a stick shift. The more successes he generated, however, the less valid his early belief became and the more valid the new belief became. "I can't do it" became "I can do it" because John was doing it.

Learned Helplessness

One of life's biggest challenges is knowing how to interpret failures, or even difficult situations and people. Sometimes we get so many references of failure that we begin to believe that nothing we do will make any situation better. Some people, when faced with difficult people and uncomfortable situations, believe they are helpless. Their reaction, as understandable as it may be, is nothing more than a way to avoid fear and to comfort their egos in the face of difficulty. When we indulge in these kinds of defense mechanisms, we block our ability to act, solve problems and mature. This destructive mind set, called "learned helplessness," is at the root of immature behavior.

John had good reasons to believe he couldn't drive a car, not the least of which was that he'd never done it. His failure reference supported this belief, even though his initial thoughts were positive. This is why positive thoughts in and of themselves are not sufficient to propel you to new levels of maturity. Positive thoughts have to be turned into firmly held beliefs by creating references that support the validity of those positive thoughts. Very little good can come from continually telling yourself, "I'm good," "I'm confident," "I'm worthy of success" and similar sentiments if the words you use are incongruent with a reference system that says the opposite. The only way to create supporting references is to create successes. And you can't create successes without taking a risk, without taking some type of action aimed at providing support for your thoughts. John initially failed in his quest to drive a stick shift, but also believed he would succeed, because people he knew had succeeded. If they had met the challenge, so could he.

Too often when people fail, they perceive their efforts as futile and develop the terminal discouragement of learned helplessness. Mature people don't allow this to happen. When mature people fail, they interpret the pain associated with their failure to be less permanent than do immature people. While immature people use words such as "always" ("It's always going to be this bad") or "never" ("It's never going to improve"), mature people see and phrase their failures as temporary setbacks. Conversely, when immature people succeed, they see their success in temporary terms. Mature people, on the other hand, interpret positive situations in permanent terms.

Another difference between mature and immature people, those who are optimistic and those who are pessimistic, is that immature people interpret their setbacks and the pain associated with those setbacks in personal terms: "It's my fault!" "I should have done this!" Or they externalize the blame for their problems: "It's your fault!" "You are responsible for this!" Mature people, on the other hand, are more optimistic and less likely to blame themselves or others. Instead, they may ask: "Why did this happen?" "What are we going to do to solve the problem?"

But How to Turn It Around?

The most effective way to change your view of who you are and who you're capable of becoming is by changing your reference system. This means you have to learn to succeed. The more success you can create — the more times you are able to step in that Volkswagen and drive it successfully — the more chances you have to interpret all your success as permanent and attributable to you. Whatever failures you suffer will be less permanent and less attributable to you. This ability to create a "more vs. less" dichotomy is based on your willingness to take reasonable risks, accept the consequences of your behavior and never give up your pursuit for success.

Easier said than done. But a good place to begin is with a positive, self-affirming value system. To value something is to place importance on it, to show genuine interest in it. If you value money, for example, you're interested in money. You tend to read about money, talk about money, look for ways to earn it, save it, invest it and spend it. And what you display interest in, you have a favorable attitude toward. This attitude moves you to act in ways that move you toward the pleasures you have learned to associate with the values you possess. Because you value some things more than others, you are also motivated to seek the pleasures of some values more than others.

Basically, there are two types of values: ultimate and intermediate. If we were to ask you, "What do you value most?" you might answer, "Love, security, independence." These are ultimate values because they are what you ultimately desire. On the other hand, if you answered, "I want money and family," these would be intermediate values because we probe further: "What will money do for you?" or "What's the importance of family in your life?"

The first, immediate challenge in the quest for greater maturity is to recognize the difference between intermediate and ultimate values, and then set for yourself goals that your ultimate values can support. This is no easy task. How many times in your life have you confused intermediate goals with ultimate goals and, once you achieved them, wound up asking, "Is this all there is?" Don't confuse setting up goals, then, with the pursuit of your ultimate values. Here, for example, is a list of some common ultimate values:

- Health and physical well-being
- Independence
- Interdependence
- Dependence
- Love
- Security
- Risk-taking
- Freedom
- Success

All nine of these values give pleasure in some way, shape, or form. But which ones do you value more? Value less? Rank them in order of importance from 1 to 9, with 1 being the most valued and 9 being the least. This hierarchy controls every decision you make and, ultimately, the degree of pleasure or pain you experience is a result of those decisions.

Type Two personalities, or Helpers, as we've seen, are much more likely to rank dependence, love and security as higher values than Type Eight, or Driver, personalities. They are more likely to value independence, risk-taking and success as their highest values. Are Helpers and Drivers different people? Of course! They have different values, beliefs, feelings, different occupations and probably even own different makes of automobiles. Remember that while your values move you in directions of known pleasure, it is your past experiences that have taught you to determine which values are most pleasurable to you. Drivers, for example, have learned from their past references that taking risks, being independent and taking control are pleasurable. Because these values are associated with pleasure, they shape every decision Drivers make and everything they do. It shapes who they establish relationships with and how those relationships will work. It also causes them to be uncomfortable in situations where they're unable to pursue the pleasures their values possess. Put an immature Driver in a situation where he or she can't drive, and you're in for a very difficult time.

Harnessing the Power in Values

Once you know your values, you can understand better why you move consistently in certain directions. By examining your hierarchy, you can see why you sometimes have a hard time making decisions or why the decisions you make sometimes cause conflict for you. Consider this: If your number-one value is security and your number-two value is risk-taking, you have polar opposite values so close in rank that you're going to experience a lot of stress when making decisions.

When you prepare to make a decision, you measure and weigh the probabilities of that decision bringing you pleasure or pain. If, for example, we asked you to go into a batting cage and try to hit baseballs thrown to you at 90 miles per hour and the number-one state that you were motivated to avoid was fear, you probably would resist going into the cage. But if your fear was the fear of rejection and you believed we would spurn you because you didn't even get in the cage, you might very well pick up a bat and face the music. Or, in this case, the fast balls. In other words, the pain you have learned to associate with your referent experiences will affect whatever decision you make. Here are some examples of emotional states many people try to avoid:

- Fear
- Anxiety
- Guilt
- Worry
- Sadness
- Anger
- Depression
- Failure
- Loneliness

All of these states are associated with pain, but which states are more painful to you? Rank these states in the order of those you'd most want to avoid (1) to those you'd least want to avoid (9). What does the ranked list now tell you? If the state you most want to avoid is fear, then you should be able to see the extent to which you avoid people and situations that make you uncomfortable.

To spiral toward greater levels of maturity, you need to alter the hierarchy of your values to support the goals you want to pursue. Note that the values to which you give a high priority are not so much the result of intelligent choices as they are the result of the experiences and values that conditioned you to live within a clearly defined system of pain and pleasure. From your Mattone Enneagram profile, you know that, while you have values that empower you and propel you upward toward greater maturity, you also have values and avoidance states that get in your way. To make the kinds of concrete changes that will enable you to become more mature, you need to create a values hierarchy that will support your new goals and actions. You need to learn to associate pain with values that limit you from becoming a mature person and associate pleasure with values that propel you to new levels of maturity.

If, for example, you value being dependent and your personality type is a Two (a Helper), yet most of your total score is tabulated by traits that reflect overdependency, your values priority is obviously in your way. To become more mature, you need to set goals that will move you away from dependence and toward interdependence. You need to learn to associate pleasure with interdependence by experiencing the pleasures that go with acting in interdependent ways.

It is this combination, then, of experiences and values that make up most of your thoughts. A mature person thinks "I can!" while an immature is immobilized by "I can't!" A mature person thinks, "I am worthy of success!" while an immature one thinks, "I am not." Why? One reason is that mature people believe in their ability to work through the challenges presented by the people and situations in their lives. This confidence wouldn't have been possible, however, without experiences to support the validity of their thoughts. Mature people, then, create success references that in turn strengthen their belief that they can be successful. This combination of continually renewed thought and action propels the person into an increasingly more mature cycle where he or she has no choice but to use positive thoughts and language.

But what about immature people? What about their language? Well, as you might expect, poor references of experience lead to poor beliefs, which lead to nonsupportive values, which lead to such negative thoughts as:

I'm a failure.

The world is treating me badly.

I'm a victim.

Nobody loves me.

Everybody judges me.

Other people are controlling my destiny.

When I speak, people better listen.

I don't need help from anybody.

The world owes me obedience.

All of these thoughts are either true or false depending on your reference of experiences. Mature people, by comparison, keep their thinking patterns positive when confronted with negative thoughts by relying on three mental processes:

1. Stress Inoculation
2. Thought-Stopping
3. Non-Negative Thinking

Stress Inoculation

Worrying about the future creates anxiety in the present, and stress inoculation reduces that anxiety. Imagine you have a performance evaluation coming up soon. Imagine also that your boss is a fast talker and poor listener (a Generalist). Prior to previous performance reviews, you've worried and become upset. To inoculate yourself this time, write a message to yourself about the situation beforehand. Address the words to yourself as if someone you admire were coaching you:

"Relax. Review your strengths and weaknesses to predict what your boss is likely to say. Be aware of discrepancies between what your manager says and what you think. Be prepared to bring these subjects up without emotion. It is possible to disagree agreeably. Rehearse your responses to anticipated feedback. Recognize that you need feedback to grow and that you are no less of a person for accepting guidance. To discourage feedback is to diminish your right to choose how you want to behave and to lose the control that comes with behavior that is attractive to others."

Once you have created your message, read it aloud several times before the actual review happens, but don't memorize it. Instead, remember its essence so you can repeat portions of it at different times during the interview and not sound rehearsed.

Thought-Stopping

Whenever you have an annoying thought running through your head, close your eyes and tell yourself: *"STOP!"* Your thought will automatically stop. Next, replace your negative thought with a positive one. The unwanted thought will probably return, but, if you patiently repeat the procedure, you will increase the time it takes to sneak back in. Here are some positive self-statements you can use to minimize the influence of negative thoughts:

Positive Self-Statements

I am good.
I am confident.
I am competent.
I am worthy of success.
I am a gifted human being.
I am respected.
I am admired.
I am a kind and loving person.
I contribute to the world.
I can deal with conflict.
I can handle anger.
I can deal with stress.
I will be the best I can be.

If only positive thoughts of and by themselves could propel us to new levels of success and maturity.... Unfortunately, we must work hard to turn these thoughts into beliefs, and the only way to do that is to create references that will support the validity of these positive thoughts. And you can't create references unless you take the risks and engage in the behavior that enables you to be certain about your thoughts as an important first step. As slow and as frustrating as this may seem to get at times, the key is to learn to repeat, rehearse and memorize your list of personal self-affirming statements. Also consider visualizing how you would act in situations where you followed through on your positive thoughts. If you say, for example, "I can handle anger," recall a time when you didn't handle your anger very well. Now visualize the specific ways you would positively work through your anger to create a far different outcome.

Non-Negative Thinking or
Learning How to Argue With Yourself

Simply put, mature people are better than immature people at disputing the validity of negative thoughts. One way they do this is by looking for proof. "What evidence justifies this thought?" When mature people hear "I never do anything right; I'm such a loser," their inner response is often something like: "Is it really true that I never do anything right?" or "What things I do well?" or "What am I not so good at?" These questions and others like them dispute the validity of negative thoughts because they are based on references to experiences that clearly verify: "I am not a loser!"

Another way to dispute the validity of negative thoughts is to look for *alternate explanations.* Very little that happens to you can be traced to one cause; most events have multiple causes. Whereas immature people will often latch onto the most dire possible belief—not because the evidence supports it but precisely because it's so dire—mature people generate a number of reasonable alternative causes to explain their setbacks.

A healthy belief system, supportive values and positive thoughts all contribute to the development of mature emotions. Because mature people know that they control their emotions, they simply choose to be happy, passionate, hopeful people in their work and in their personal lives. They then strengthen their emotions by making yet another important choice: When faced with a difficult situation or an encounter with a difficult person, mature people create a mental map that they can follow to success. Through the powers of your imagination, you can learn to mentally map your way to experiencing emotions that will empower you to act in mature ways. If, for example, one of your goals is to become a better team player, you may wish to list some past experiences where not being a team member led to failure. Perhaps you were afraid to offer your opinions to the team or perhaps someone on a team stole your ideas, whatever. The point of this exercise is to reinforce the concept that when you're not doing what you could be doing to become more mature, you're creating an experience of failure that will lead to more failure if you don't change. Here's a brief list of the key points:

- Ask yourself what happened to cause the failure.
- Visualize the details of the situation (i.e., the who's, what's, when's, where's, why's and how's), as painful as they may be.
- Compare how you felt then with how you feel now.
- What did you do to handle this situation? Did submitting to others or becoming aggressive serve to solve the problem?
- Review in your mind the details of your response: your thoughts, your words, your tone of voice.
- Now decide what you want to change about your response to avoid similar experiences in the future.

Once you've mapped out a failure scenario, you need to visualize a situation — even if you have very few references to support it — where being a better team member will lead to feelings of excitement, exhilaration, power and success. Imagine yourself offering ideas to your team members, solving problems with your team members, getting recognition for your contributions, growing as a result of your opening up and listening to alternative viewpoints, and enjoying the success that comes from being a part of a winning team. Again, the point is to strengthen the association that acting on your developmental goal of becoming a better team player will lead to pleasure. The more references you have to support this belief, the stronger the association. As you did in the failure scenario, visualize the details of the imagined situation and picture yourself handling team situations effectively. See successful results, an award for quality service, for example, then visualize and rehearse the steps you need to take to make those pictures real. The more you rehearse these steps, the stronger your association will be that the new behavior is pleasurable and the old behavior is not. The positive emotional state you've created in your mind now becomes the impetus for the positive actions that will take place in reality.

Note: All great achievers are visualizers. They see it; they feel it; they experience it before they actually do it. In other words, they begin with where they want to end. You can do the same in every area of your life. Mature people mentally map out their success in their work, whether it be a sales presentation, a difficult confrontation, meeting a tough goal or dealing with downsizing in their organization. They see their success clearly and vividly, and they repeat and rehearse their success picture until it becomes an integral part of who they are. Then, when they experience the actual situation, they are already empowered to act in mature, problem-solving ways.

Ways is the key word here. In the age of accelerating change and complexity, you want to be versatile. Versatility is independent of personality type; it is also a measure of social endorsement. People who have learned how to meet the demands of others in a wide variety of situations will, more often than not, receive support and endorsement from those they've helped. On the other hand, those who have been less resourceful in meeting the varied needs of others will often receive less support and endorsement. To be versatile is to observe and empathize. The better you are able to recognize others' needs and empathize with their emotions, the better you'll be able to relate to them and the more effectively mature you will be as a person. Here are some starting points:

● Try to be more pleasant; smile.

- Remember other people's names.
- Ask questions about their interests.
- Listen to what they say.
- Support what you hear.

You will note that all of these skills are part of the social repertoire of all versatile people. Their life theme is: "What can I do to make it easier for another person to relate to me?"

One place to look for an initial answer to this question is in areas of commonality. Versatile people search their experience for whatever ideas or events they might have in common with people they wish to relate to. The more they can find to share, the greater the probability of effective communication. In the diagram below, the speaker (S) and the listener (L) share varying amounts of commonality.

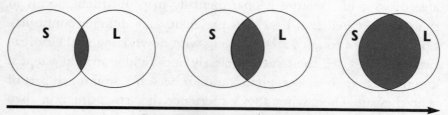

Increasing Commonality

To the extent that the speaker and the listener share more interests, they achieve greater levels of communication. Ironically, the levels of nonverbal communication increase with the increasing number of shared interests. Gestures come to take the place of many words. And this is how it should be. Nonverbal communication is simpler and often less likely to be misunderstood because it emerges straight from feelings. Uncluttered, uncomplicated and uncontaminated by thought, it represents the authentic self.

To reach this level of communication, versatile people know that the initial encounters with others often necessitate modifying their style to prepare a face to meet the faces that they meet without becoming a phony. What makes this skill so difficult to master is the inner tension that's created when you temporarily abandon your comfortable style to assume one more fitting to the situation. Fortunately, whatever modifications you make in your style are only temporary. When commonality is achieved, you can gradually return to the ways with which you are most comfortable.

The alternative to style modification is not to make the effort to adjust, to label as wrong or inferior what often is merely different. Labeling, an immature reaction designed to avoid the tension that comes with having to make changes, saves us a lot of work. Unfortunately, it also limits our ability to be flexible and, in some cases, carries the name of prejudice.

Modifying your style to relate better with others begins with the decision to accept others' styles as just as legitimate and authentic as our own. The next step is to stretch our style to include qualities common to those to which we wish to relate better. It's not much different from being a movie director. We "cast" ourselves into a role and coach ourselves just as a director would coach an actor. An Analyzer, relating to an Entertainer, might say, for example: "Don't come on too strong now. Don't dominate the scene totally. Give the other person a chance. Ask some questions. Be more objective. Draw him or her out."

An Entertainer, on the other hand, might approach an Analyzer this way: "Don't be too critical now. Assert yourself a little more. Put a little feeling into it. Remember the tendency to come on strong with lists of half-formed ideas. Bite your tongue; be less judgmental, more understanding." This doesn't necessarily mean that we must all become Entertainers; what it means is that we have to communicate in ways that are more palatable to the Entertainer behavior type; that we have to discover, understand and respond to the emotional needs of others if we want to increase our chances of effective communication.

To be truly versatile, then, is to give more to others than might be expected of us. We may not always succeed but, more often than not, we'll get points for trying. And the more we try, the better we'll get at it. In other words, true versatility and maturity know no limits. They are not tied to personality types.

Your job — now that you've identified through the Enneagram the type of person you are — is to use the Enneagram to change the degree of maturity you exhibit as part of your personality. Diversity, whether in people or situations, will always be. When you develop the ability to mature within your basic personality type, you ultimately mature beyond it to possess forever the ability to accept and relate to diversity and to create for yourself the success you so richly deserve in life.

Bibliography

Boyett, Joseph H., and Henry P. Conn. *Workplace Love*. New York: Plume, 1992.

Cameron, Norman. *Personality Development and Psychopathology*. Boston: Houghton–Mifflin, 1963.

Diagnostic and Statistical Manual of Mental Disorders. 3rd ed. Washington, D.C.: American Psychiatric Association, 1980.

Galbraith, John Kenneth. *The Anatomy of Power*. Boston: Houghton–Mifflin, 1983.

Goldenson, Robert M. *The Encyclopedia of Human Behavior*. New York: Dell, 1970.

Keen, Sam. "Interviews with Oscar Ichazo." Reprinted from *Psychology Today* (July 1973). New York: Arica Institute Press, 1982.

Korda, Michael. *Power!* New York: Random House, 1975.

Lilly, John, and Joseph Hart. "The Arica Training." In *Transpersonal Psychologies*, edited by Charles T. Tart. New York: Harper & Row, 1975.

Macquarrie, John. *In Search of Humanity*. New York: Crossroad, 1985.

Maslow, Abraham. *The Further Reaches of Human Nature*. New York: Viking Press, 1971.

Metzner, Ralph. *Know Your Type: Maps of Identity*. New York: Doubleday, 1979.

Palmer, Helen. *The Enneagram*. San Francisco: Harper & Row, 1988.

Seligman, Martin E. P. *Learned Optimism: How to Change Your Mind and Your Life*. New York: Simon and Schuster, 1990.

Speeth, Kathleen Reorden. *The Gurdjieff Work*. Berkeley: And/Or Press, 1976.

Waldberg, Michael. *Gurdjieff, An Approach to His Ideas*. London: Routledge and Keegan Paul, 1981.

About the Authors

John Mattone is one of America's leading industrial psychologists and top-rated speakers. As founder and president of Mattone Enterprises, Mattone delivers more than 100 presentations a year to such clients as: AT&T, BIC, Canadian Broadcasting Corporation, Days Inn, Citicorp, Detroit Edison, Ernst & Young, Florida Power & Light, Howard Johnson's, National Board of Realtors and Nestle. The author of *Positive Performance Management*, Mattone has designed and performed in several award-winning audio and video training programs.

Richard Andersen, Ph.D., is an award-winning college educator, a former Fulbright Professor and a James Thurber Writer-in-Residence. He is also a TV talk-show host and prolific author, with more than 15 published books to his credit. His nationally acclaimed examination of contemporary education, *Arranging Deck Chairs on the Titanic: Crisis in Education*, was called one of the best books ever written on the subject and was chosen for a PBS special on teachers.